The Game Show Handbook

David Mason has worked for Thames Television for the past fifteen years. Soon after joining Thames in 1976 he wrote and appeared in the children's comedy series *You Must Be Joking*. He then wrote the documentary about the Dakota aircraft *The DC3*, which was shown on the ITV network in 1982. The same year David joined the Thames Television Light Entertainment Department working on *This is Your Life*, which involved travelling all over the world for six years researching stories for the programme. In the summer months when *This is Your Life* was off the air, he worked on game shows including *Whose Baby?*, *Headliners* and *What's My Line?* In 1988 he wrote and produced the prestigious six-part photography series *Nocon on Photography*. Afterwards he returned to the Light Entertainment Department to work on many game and variety shows. In 1989 David bec⸺ ⸺ ⸺ci-
⸺t⸺ ⸺

GW00384101

DAVID MASON

DAVID N. MASON

The

Game

Show

Handbook

with a foreword by
Michael Barrymore

Thames Mandarin

To Rosemary

A Thames Mandarin Paperback
THE GAME SHOW HANDBOOK

First published in Great Britain 1991
by Mandarin Paperbacks
Michelin House, 81 Fulham Road, London SW3 6RB
in association with
Thames Television International Limited
149 Tottenham Court Road, London W1P 9LL

Mandarin is an imprint of the Octopus Publishing Group,
a division of Reed International Books Limited

Copyright © Thames Television plc
and David N. Mason 1991

The author has asserted his moral rights

A CIP catalogue record for this title
is available from the British Library
ISBN 0 7493 0904 0

Typeset by Falcon Typographic Art Ltd,
Edinburgh & London
Printed and bound in Great Britain
by Cox & Wyman Ltd, Reading, Berkshire

Contents

_____

_____

_____

_____

Acknowledgements

Without the help of the following people this book would have been impossible to write:

Michael Barrymore, Cheryl Barrymore, Margaret Bawden, Jeremy Beadle, John Bishop, Caroline Blackadder, Jim Bowen, Jim Bowie, Max Bygraves, Nicky Campbell, Jane Carr, Bobby Charlton, Jilly Cooper, Leo Cooper, James Corsan, Leslie Crowther, Paul Daniels, Eric Davidson, Les Dennis, Michael Dennison, Sara Drake, David Elias, David Elstein, Paula Eatough, John Fisher, Bruce Forsyth, Larry Grayson, Hughie Green, Anthony Gruner, David Jacobs, Gorden Kaye, Brian Klein, Stephen Leahy, Maurice Leonard, Helen Lott, Bob Louis, Peter Mason, Peter Massey, Desi Maxim, Antonia McMeeking, Jenny Moir, Bob Monkhouse, Malcolm Morris, Des O'Connor, Nicholas Parsons, Brian Penders, Pauline Quennell, Angela Rippon, Revd David Smith, Bill Stewart, Tony Vick, Gail Watkins, Colin Williams, Bernie Winters and all my colleagues and friends at Thames Television who have been bored rigid over the past year with this special project!

It took a year to write *The Game Show Handbook* and I am indebted to all the contributors I interviewed. Many of my interviews took place in very awkward situations invariably before or after television appearances in various dressing rooms at various television studios up and down the country during 1990. I am very grateful for all their help. I must give special thanks to Michael Barrymore for all his help and encouragement in the writing of the book and for agreeing to write the foreword. Special thanks must also go to Bob Monkhouse for all his enthusiastic help, advice and anecdotes. My good friend and colleague, Maurice Leonard, being a much respected author in his own right, gave me so much encouragement with this project and I would like to say a special sincere thank you to him. I worked with Jilly Cooper on thirty-two *What's my Line* programmes in 1990 and I would like to thank her for simply saying 'What a brilliant idea – you must write it.'

Finally I must thank, on pain of death, my wife, Rosemary, who didn't see me for months on end while I was typing away in my study. Rosey is a walking dictionary and I must thank her for correcting my atrocious spelling and for proofreading manuscript after manuscript.

Foreword

_____

_____

_____

_____

Dear Reader,

Well it's too late now – you have bought the book, or is it a present, or are you just standing in the shop flicking through the pages to save you buying it? If it's the last put it down right now or go and buy it. Decisions, decisions. Lots of decisions are made by the contestants you see on game or quiz shows. The decision to apply first of all, then the decision on what is the correct answer to maybe the jackpot question . . . that's if you've got that far. Getting that far is a combination of so many things; mainly luck and all the helpful advice you can acquire. So read on, Macduff, this is the book that will help you through the climb to being a star for a night!! Your winnings could be high or low, depending on how good you are. You could come away with a _Blankety Blank_ cheque book and pen or maybe £3,000 . . . remember the better you are the higher your winnings could be.

Why was I asked to write this foreword? I suppose it's something to do with the fact that Dave, along with Maurice Leonard (The Producer) and myself have been responsible for bringing _Strike it Lucky_ to your screens

© Thames TV

for the last six years. I do the last bit . . . run down the stairs, talk to the six contestants I'd just met and try my best to encourage them to reveal talents that were so far unseen by the public, and finally help them on their way to a very large jackpot.

The hard part was done by Dave and Maurice. They auditioned thousands of people, spending months going around the country selecting contestants. Then they helped and informed the chosen few through to 'pay day'. Dave Mason knows all the answers to how these types of shows are put together, from start to finish.

So I will finish and let you enjoy, and hopefully gain, from reading this book.

Alwight!

Introduction

Game shows are fun, and in some cases a lot of money can be won for just a few minutes' work. There are many reasons why people like to participate in game shows. For some it is the money, for others it is the fun of doing it, for some it is a challenge and for others it is the fame. Whatever your reasons you have strong competition to get on the screen. However, it has to be said that anybody can apply to appear on any game show.

All game shows require contestants and it really doesn't matter if you are black, white, tall, short, fat, thin, old, young, or disabled in some way, everyone stands a chance. In the past this may not have been the case, but attitudes are changing and, as a producer, I would give equal consideration to everyone who applied. Provided they want to participate and pass the audition, then why shouldn't they go on the show? For disability look at the 1989 *Mastermind* series when Mary-Elizabeth Raw who was wheelchair-bound won the final. For sheer guts, look at the 1990 series of *Strike it Lucky* when Arthur Haddock went across the arches pressing the buttons while his wife answered the questions. Arthur was totally blind. I cried when they won the jackpot of £3,000. I feel that possibly people who don't fit the imaginary criteria of a game show contestant do not apply for shows. If you want to go on a show, then apply! How else are producers to know who wants to take part?

Having said that, there are thousands of people in this country who, like you, would like to participate. But how do you go about getting on to a show? There is a standard route, but along the way there are many pitfalls!

I have been involved in many game shows over the fifteen years I have worked for Thames Television and, at times, the job of choosing contestants has been a most frustrating experience. Game show producers spend roughly half their year auditioning contestants from a supply which may exceed demand by as much as 150 to 1. It became obvious to me while we were auditioning in 1989 for *Strike it Lucky* that many hopefuls didn't understand the selection system and indeed didn't know what would be expected of them when they auditioned. Many fell at the first hurdle when they failed to fill in the application form correctly. Others sent in ridiculous or even obscene photographs with their completed forms while others made complete fools of themselves at the audition.

But what makes a good contestant? What do producers look for? How do you apply for a show? How do you choose which show you would like to appear on? How do you fill in an application form? What is a contestants' audition? What happens during the recording of a game show? These are all questions that will be answered in the following chapters.

The object of this handbook is to guide you through the relatively simple process of getting on to a game show with advice from those who have successfully done so in the past. The book is punctuated with tips and anecdotes from hosts, producers and contestant researchers from many of the major shows on TV today.

After reading the book you should feel a little more confident about having a go and applying for a show. So get reading, get writing, and get lucky!

David Mason
East Molesey,
December 1990

One

A

Brief History

of

Game Shows

Television was invented by a Scotsman, John Logie Baird, in 1926, and heralded the dramatic shift of entertainment from the music halls, theatres and cinemas to the living-room. It was a world with glittering opportunities, and soon the screens flickered with news, plays, variety shows, children's programmes . . . and game shows.

The very first TV game show was *Spelling Bee* shown by the BBC on 31 May 1938. As with all early programmes it was transmitted live from Alexandra Palace, the home of BBC television for many years. It graduated from radio and was a simple spelling game hosted by the broadcaster, Freddie Grisewood. He would ask the first member of the panel something like: 'Spell a word meaning extremely numerous. It is INNUMERABLE.' If the word was spelt incorrectly then Freddie would pass it on to the next panellist to try and so on until someone spelt it correctly and thus scored a point.

That really must have been the most boring show ever dreamt up!

Records indicate that the first regular television game show, and the longest running one, is *What's My Line?*

This started life in 1950 in the USA and was first seen in Great Britain in 1951 with Eamonn Andrews in the chair. The show is still running after forty years but now with Angela Rippon inviting the next contestant to 'Sign in, please'.

Headmaster Freddie Grisewood tests the spelling abilities of Margaretta Scott in *Spelling Bee*. © BBC

The original *What's My Line?* panel had some famous regulars: Gilbert Harding, Isobel Barnett and Barbara Kelly. Actor Michael Denison was a regular panellist in 1953, and he remembered the show with great affection when he recently returned to it as the mystery celebrity. Nowadays four shows are recorded a day over an eight-day period, unlike forty years ago when the programmes were transmitted live. 'Things were much more leisurely then,' recalled Michael. The panel and chairman may have changed but the show still manages to be famous for finding the odd occupations from a toilet flush assembler to the man who sells seawater for a living! The most famous of all odd occupations must have been a couple of years ago when we managed to find a sagger maker bottom knocker. 'What is it?' you may well ask, as did our panel. Apparently, in pottery making the item to be fired rests in the kiln on a piece of ceramic, called a sagger. This chap actually made the sagger and also had the job of removing the sagger after firing by knocking it off the pot. Invariably the sagger was attached to the bottom of the piece, hence the job title!

Isobel Barnett, Michael Denison, Barbara Kelly and Gilbert Harding on *What's My Line?* in 1953. © S. & G. Press Agency

In the series that we recorded in June 1990 with regular panellists Jilly Cooper and Roy Hudd the contestant who had the panel guessing the most, and had the audience in fits of laughter, was Arthur Wainwright from Huddersfield. His occupation was that of surgical shaver. He worked at the Huddersfield Royal Infirmary but unfortunately he had broken his arm, so that although it usually takes about three seconds to 'Sign in' it took him about thirty, and his writing was very shaky! He did his mime — which was rather explicit — but had the panel fooled, and he beat them. 'What were you doing in your mime?' asked Angela Rippon, reminding him it was a family show. 'I was shaving a gentleman's private parts,' replied Arthur, 'and I use an ordinary safety razor with a new blade every Monday and God help you on Thursday!'

I doubt very much if Eamonn Andrews would have had Arthur on the show as he was a man of strong principles and he wouldn't have thought Arthur's occupation was one to laugh about. There are a few famous incidents written about Eamonn in the annals of television. For instance, the *What's My Line?* panel, blindfolded for this spot on the show, have to guess the identity of a mystery celebrity who disguises his voice when answering their questions. Picking the celebrity was an exercise fraught with danger, as Eamonn had definite ideas as to who they should be.

On one famous occasion the producer approached Hollywood legend Charlton Heston. After a lot of begging and persuasion Mr Heston agreed to do the show even though he was visiting England for only a very short time. Eamonn flew off the handle and said, 'Is there no one else available who's better known?' The producer replied that the only other celebrity available was Acker Bilk, to which Eamonn replied, 'Now you're talking'! Eamonn did have his favourites and Acker was one of them.

What's My Line? has no great prizes to offer but it was, and still is, a very popular show. The only reward to anyone who beats the panel is a certificate to say you have done so.

The real money-spinning game shows were introduced in the early 1950s in the United States. Probably the most famous of all was *The $64,000 Question*. This half-hour quiz started life on 7 June 1955 and, like many television programmes at the time, was based on a radio show called *Take It or Leave It* which had a top prize of just $64,

Angela Rippon asks *What's My Line?* © Thames TV

made up from the questions doubling in value from $1 as the contestant answered them. The first person to win the grand TV prize was a Richard McCutchen on the subject of cooking. To win the prize he had to answer the final question: 'Name and describe five dishes and two wines from the menu of a royal banquet given in 1939 by King George VI of England for French President Albert Lebrun.' (*Everyone* knows that!) His answer was consommé, quenelles, filet de truite saumonée, petits pois à la française, sauce maltaise and corbeille. The two wines were Château d'Yquem and Madeira Sercial. As a gag, the American comedian Jack Benny (renowned for being very careful with his money) went on to the show as a contestant; he answered the first question, on the subject of the violin, and quit with his winnings of one dollar!

In true American style more money was offered in a development of the original idea in a show called *The $64,000 Challenge*, where contestants could challenge winners from *The $64,000 Question* who had won at least $8,000. The show was first broadcast on 8 April 1956 and the biggest money winner was Teddy Nadler from St Louis with $252,000. One producer wanted to up the prize money again so he called the show *The $128,000 Question*. That show ran for two years from 1976 to 1978. One of the biggest problems was its title . . . try saying 'The $128,000 Question'! With such big prizes rumours became rife that the shows were rigged in order to let popular contestants go on week after week and hence increase the ratings. The scandal was confirmed when a contestant, who won $129,000 on a show called 21 confessed to a Grand Jury in 1959 that he was told the answers. This was known as the '1958 quiz scandal' and because of this that particular show was dropped after a run of ten years.

Viewers to ITV will know that in 1990 *The $64,000 Question* was revived with great success, and with ratings to match. Bob Monkhouse who asks the questions, likes to call it 'Mastermind with Money' but, unlike America, the top prize on offer is just £6,400. 'Why didn't you change the title?' I asked Bob and he told me, 'You don't fool around with successful catchphrases. The show is still the same food but with different gravy!' In this country the amount of prize-money is currently limited by the Independent Television Commission (ITC). The transmission time of the show dictates how much money can be given away. At the moment it is about £5,000 maximum per peak-time show but this can be accumulated over a period. For instance, there may be a jackpot that can increase in value if it isn't won. From 1993, though, the limits for prizes will be abolished and programme sponsorship will be allowed; there could be rich pickings for all contestants, but let's hope there isn't a quiz scandal in this country!

An important date and time in Britain's television history came on 22 September 1955 at 7.15 p.m., for it was then that ITV began broadcasting. The programme that launched the new network was a banquet at the Guildhall, London. Viewers were on the edge of their seats one hour later, for it was then that the first television commercial was seen. (It was for Gibbs SR Toothpaste – a good Trivial Pursuit question.) Two major quiz shows took to the air in Britain on the new commercial network: *Double Your Money* on Wednesday nights and *Take Your Pick* on Friday nights. These shows are very important in the history of game shows for they were the first to offer cash prizes on British television. Both of them graduated from radio, having been heard for three years on Radio Luxembourg before transferring to television.

It has been said that *Double Your Money* was based on *The $64,000 Question* but its host, Canadian ex-pilot Hughie Green, is adamant that this was not the case. He told me that it was in existence well before *The $64,000 Question*. However, it was the first in this country to offer a prize of £1,000 . . . a lot of money in 1955! Hughie Green was always assisted by a lady, the most famous of all being the young 'Cheeky Cockney', Monica Rose, who got the job after being such a success as a contestant on the show. The show broke new ground in this area for this was the first time that lady hostesses were allowed to talk on game shows. Prior to this they were used as 'dressing' but now the ladies' personalities were allowed to shine through. Many television viewers will remember Monica Rose but may have forgotten the other female assistants including the lady with the fuller figure, Sabrina, as well as Nancy Roberts and Jean Clark. Probably the most famous contestant who appeared on *Double Your Money* was footballer Bobby Charlton who won £1,000 answering questions on pop music.

Take Your Pick was hosted by 'your quiz inquisitor' Michael Miles. The game required little skill. Contestants were chosen from the studio audience and were initially subjected to the infamous 'Yes/No' interlude where Michael quizzed his contestants for one minute with simple questions about themselves but they could neither answer yes or no nor nod or shake their heads. They returned to answer three simple general knowledge questions. If they got these questions right – and they usually did! – they were invited to pick a key to a box. They were offered money for the key which, if refused, enabled the contestant to open a box and win the prize inside. The prizes ranged from booby prizes (for example, a used tea bag) to star prizes of trips around the world. However, the top prize wasn't always a trip around the world. On one vintage show I saw recently the top prize was two weeks in Hastings, and some of the other prizes on offer included a Braille washing machine and a transistor radio combined with a camera so you could take pictures while listening to your favourite radio show!

I can remember being amused at the way Hughie Green and Michael Miles used to have a friendly on-screen

Do you want to open the box or take the money?
Michael Miles asked you to 'Take your pick'. © Thames TV

rivalry as they tried to put each other down. On one show a booby prize was a ticket to see *Double Your Money* being made! Both shows were axed in 1968. In 1991 it was announced that *Take Your Pick* was to be revived by Thames Television with Des O'Connor as presenter.

For David Jacobs 1955 was definitely the year of the ITV game show. The popular television and radio presenter had two games in the top three most popular programmes: *Tell the Truth* and *Make Up Your Mind*.

Make Up Your Mind was a valuation quiz made by Granada Television in Manchester and achieved very high ratings. The basic idea was that an object was displayed together with a sum of money. The contestants had to determine what was more valuable; the money or the object. If they guessed correctly then they won either the money or the object, whatever was the more valuable. Sometimes really strange objects were brought on, and David remembers a live leopard being the subject of valuation. The programme was live and made in front of a studio audience and naturally audience, contestants and David were all concerned about their own safety with this wild animal roaming around. They were all assured by the handler that if everyone kept very quiet all would be OK. The game was duly played but as the animal was being put back into its cage the doors of the studio flew open and hundreds of students collecting money for their rag week invaded the studio rattling collecting tins and waving banners. Fortunately the animal was quickly caged up but, as David says, 'Had the students burst in just a few seconds earlier they might have all been eaten!'

Tell the Truth, the game where three contestants claim to be someone but only one of them is the real person, was made by ATV (Associated Television) at the Hackney Empire in London. It ran from 1955 to 1959 with David in the chair but then he left to host *Juke Box Jury*. (Incidentally, David told me that *Juke Box Jury* was meant to have only a very short run, but it turned out to be so popular that it ran non-stop every Saturday evening for eight and a half years!) *Tell the Truth* is a game show chestnut as it can still be seen today, albeit during the daytime unlike the 1950s when it was a peak-time show.

The 1960s saw game shows develop alongside advances in technology as they became 'high-tech'. Probably the best example of this was *The Golden Shot*. This show started life in Switzerland and was inspired by none other than William Tell. It hit British screens in 1967 and involved contestants taking part in competitive crossbow shooting for prizes. Contestants had to qualify over the telephone by verbally directing the aim of a blindfolded crossbow shooter. Attached to the crossbow was a camera and the viewer, by watching his television, could thus direct the aim. After qualifying over the telephone contestants would go to the studio the following week to compete by aiming and shooting the crossbows themselves. On one famous occasion it was discovered that a contestant wasn't phoning from his home but from a telephone box and was directing the crossbow by watching the show on a television screen across the road in a Visionhire shop!

After the transmission slot was shifted from Saturday evenings to Sunday tea time, the show, then hosted by Bob Monkhouse, attracted over 17 million viewers. The show was live fifty-two weeks of the year and Bob remembers that it was punctuated with disasters.

> 'Something went wrong on every show. The trouble with *The Golden Shot* was that it went out live. One week a contestant disappeared from the studio and she went to the lavatory just as she was about to go on. While she was on the loo she suddenly heard her name called, jumped to her feet and knocked herself out on the loo door!'

Contestants seemed to make a habit of disappearing from
the set. On another famous occasion two contestants, after
competing in the first round of firing crossbows in the studio, were led away by the floor assistant to wait for the next
round – but they disappeared (some think they went to the
loo or just went wandering off – the studio was a maze of

Young Bob Monkhouse scored a bullseye
with *The Golden Shot*. © Central TV

corridors, and remember the show was live), so when
the time came for the next round the enterprising floor
manager dragged two total strangers out of the audience
and Bob, the ever-professional host, referred to them by
the same names as the people who had disappeared.
They went on to win and were given handsome gifts
and hundreds of pounds and not one viewer telephoned
the studios to say that the contestants had changed!

The 1970s had us glued to our sets every week watching

the suave Nicholas Parsons hosting the show that was introduced by the words, 'From Norwich, it's the quiz of the week – the *Sale of the Century*'. Made by Anglia Television, it was one of the most popular quizzes on television and ran from 1971 to 1984 before being resurrected on satellite television in 1989 with Peter Marshall as host. The game had three contestants answering increasingly difficult questions and using their scores to buy discounted goods. Nicholas Parsons remembers one woman who when asked 'What is a billet-doux' replied, 'It's something you sit on – a sort of lavatory'!

Audiences in the 1970s were soon being treated to personality game shows where the personality of both the host and the contestants mattered as much to the programme as the game itself. For instance, in 1971 a Dutch idea was bought by Bill Cotton, the controller of light entertainment at the BBC, and put on to our screens. The Dutch title was 'Een Van De Aacht'. We knew it better as *The Generation Game*. Hosted by Bruce Forsyth, the show was an instant success and introduced new phrases in to the English language like 'Give us a twirl', 'Didn't he do well' as well as making sure that he would never forget to mention the 'cuddly toy'. Like the cuddly toy, the prizes were quite meagre compared to today's standards but the personality of the host and that of the contestants were more important than the prizes.

Bruce told me that he learned his craft of audience participation while performing in a 1950s summer season at Babbacombe. The rules dictated that on a Sunday no props or scenery could be used, so Bruce, always the improviser, ingeniously used people instead! This is how his ability of using the audience on stage was discovered. It was a natural talent.

After Bruce left the show Larry Grayson brought *The Generation Game* back on our screens in 1977 and its success continued bringing even more unique phrases

Host of *Sale of the Century* Nicholas Parsons
assisted by Karen Loughlin and Carole Ashby. © Anglia TV

into everyday use, like 'Let's see the scores on the doors' and 'Look at the muck in 'ere'. If you can remember Larry hosting the game then you will remember that he always had guests behind the doors. 'Who is the star behind the door tonight' he used to say, opening it. Larry says that for the four years he hosted the show they never got the doors right. They always used to get stuck and he couldn't open them, leaving stars like Jessie Matthews trying to squeeze through a small gap.

In 1990 the show was revived with original host Bruce Forsyth putting contestants through the most ridiculous ordeals in order to win a toaster, but even so the viewing public still love it and it is again one of the most popular shows on television today.

Larry Grayson reappeared on our screens in 1987 with a show from Anglia Television called *Sweethearts*. Occasionally shows do bomb and this was one of them. Hilary Kingsley and Geoff Tibballs say about it in their marvellous book on television, *Box of Delights*, '. . . *Sweethearts*, the who's-telling-the-truth-about-their-romance guessing game, was supposed to be Larry Grayson's comeback but was more of a coffin.'

'No, it wasn't a success,' says Larry. 'They put us up against *EastEnders* and the show was made in Norwich, miles from anywhere right in the middle of the countryside. Larry says that he doesn't like television game shows anymore: there are too many of them. He says that even his brown poodle is terrified of them. Every time a questionmaster asks a question on a quiz show the dog runs and hides!

In 1972 a unique event took place in the history of British television quizzes. A quiz show which was inspired by none other than Hitler was moved to a peak-time slot because at the last minute a play about Casanova which was considered too risqué had to be rescheduled and something had to fill the space. The replacement was a very difficult quiz which was soon regularly attracting over 20 million viewers. Unlike other quiz programmes the only prize on offer was a glass bowl. *Mastermind* has been with us ever since and still remains a firm favourite with the British viewers.

Icelandic quizmaster Magnus Magnusson has put the questions since show one. Some of the specialist subjects chosen by contestants have been quite unusual (such as the life cycle of the honey bee) but some have been so specialized that they couldn't be used, for instance: beers of the world, routes to anywhere in mainland Britain from Letchworth, and Siamese cats since 1875! Why inspired by Hitler? Bill Wright, the BBC producer who thought up the idea, was in the air force during World War II and was shot down over Holland. He became a prisoner and was often interrogated by the Germans. The only information he was allowed to impart during interrogation was name, rank and number, but it was from his experience of being in a dark room with a light shining on him and being asked questions that the idea came to him (some years later!) for *Mastermind*. Instead of name rank and number it is now name, occupation and subject. Mrs Jennifer Keaveney scored a record 40 points answering questions on the life and works of E. Nesbit in a 1986 semi-final. She scored another 40 points when she won the final answering questions on the life and works of Elizabeth Gaskell. This record was almost equalled in the 1989 series when Mary-Elizabeth Raw scored 40 points on the life and reign of Charles I. Mary went on to win the final.

The BBC were having great success with *The Generation Game* in the late 1970s and ITV desperately needed something that would offer some competition. Yorkshire Television found the ideal show in Spain. There it was called 'Un Dos Tres' (One, two, three); all YTV did was change the title to *3–2–1* and they had an instant hit. The show was made in Leeds and was hosted by comic Ted Rogers, who put devious clues

Winner of the 1989 *Mastermind* Mary-Elizabeth Raw being presented with the *Mastermind* trophy by previous winner Fred Housego as questionmaster Magnus Magnusson looks on. © BBC

to his contestants to help them unravel mysteries after they had watched sketches and heard jokes. Personally, I found the whole show a mystery and never really did understand it. Eric Davidson, who worked on it as a writer for a number of years, told me that he's not surprised I found it confusing as the contestants did as well! He told me that the show took three hours to record and the contestants had to hang around becoming more and more nervous as the evening wore on. Sometimes they would forget the clues simply because it took so long to go from one section of the programme to another. 'Some were jittering wrecks by the end of the evening,' said Eric. Personally I was totally confused as to why the star of the show wasn't Ted but a motorized dustbin! However, I was in the minority for the show enjoyed ten years at the top, regularly attracting over 16 million viewers.

During the 1980s the screens burst forth with new shows, but only a few of those are still going today.

Bullseye, the game of darts and general knowledge, is still going strong hosted by Jim ('Smashing, great') Bowen. It was in 1981 that *Bullseye* moved Jim from stand-up comedy shows to the role of quizmaster. That transition can be very difficult, for Jim told me that on the early shows he was concentrating more on the camera movements, and where he should be looking, rather than on what his contestants were saying to him. For instance, this particular piece of dialogue with a contestant named Ken has become one of television's great moments:

> JIM: Hello Ken, and what do you do for a living?
> KEN: I'm unemployed, Jim.
> JIM: Smashin', Ken, loovely.

Jim is a great guy and much respected in the entertainment industry. I really enjoyed researching his story for *This Is*

Your Life in 1985, when many other stories about *Bullseye* came out. Like the famous occasion when he read out the question immediately followed by the answer, but we won't mention that! Frank Carson told us on Jim's 'life' that no one has ever won the car on *Bullseye* so when it is eventually won the first thing the winners will have to do is get an MOT for it!

If there isn't a car to be won then there is invariably a speed boat. 'That's a lot of use if you live in Nuneaton!' comments Jim.

The longest running daytime network TV game show in the United States became a hit for peak-time television here. On Saturday 24 March 1984 *The Price is Right* had Leslie Crowther as host inviting contestants to 'Come on down' to guess the retail price of goods on offer. The nearest to the right price won the goods. Like *Take Your Pick*, the contestants were chosen from the studio audience, an exercise that can be fraught with danger. On the very first *The Price is Right* a contestant was invited to 'Come on down' and she refused! A man from Brixton won a holiday for two, making a girl from Liverpool the loser. The winner stunned everyone by promptly asking her to go along on the holiday. Leslie told me that Bill Stewart, now known as presenter, William G. Stewart of *Fifteen to One* fame, was the producer of the programme and would choose the contestants. He used to appear to the sound of 'Land of Hope and Glory' played at a deafening level and then get all the audience to sing it as loud as they could. After this rather grand entrance he would chat to the audience and talk to the individual coach parties. He used a special codeword in his patter so that his assistant would know which members of the audience he would get Leslie to invite to 'Come on down'.

Many successful shows use celebrities for both contestants and panellists. For example, *Whose Baby?*. This programme was devised by Eamonn Andrews and involved celebrity panellists guessing the identity of famous parents by questioning the offspring. The most recent host was Bernie Winters. I interviewed Bernie a year before his untimely death when he jokingly told me that the powers

Producer Bill Stewart and host Leslie Crowther with two contestants they invited to 'Come on down'. © Central TV

that be at Thames Television called him in one day to offer him the job. He was told that it required pathos and humility and as far as they were concerned Bernie was the most pathetic and humiliating person they knew, so he got it! As I am sure you know, Bernie always had his dog Schnorbitz with him, and *Whose Baby?* was no exception; the large St Bernard was always by his side on the set. The children loved the dog, but as the old showbiz adage goes, never work with children or animals . . . with *Whose Baby?* we had both. Invariably the dog was the star of the show for not turning a hair (or baring a tooth) after being mauled by hundreds of children and cooed over by hundreds of adults. Schnorbitz always ate sausages and so we had to have pounds of the things on hand to keep the 'star' happy.

Whose Baby? host Bernie Winters with 'babysitter' Sarah Hollamby and Schnorbitz. © Thames TV

Another example of this type of show is *Through the Keyhole*. Presented by David Frost, it is a great programme for the nosey British public. Here, Loyd Grossman, a North American with trouble sounding his vowels, is filmed sifting through personal effects in the houses of well-known people, after which he puts the question to the celebrity panel, 'Who lives in a place like this?' The panel deliberate and more often than not come up with the right answer. It is a great show. I love looking at celebrities' houses but the producers could possibly have trouble finding enough celebrities willing to have their personal life blown open to the general public. We'll see.

A world-wide quiz took to the air on 17 January 1982. It was called *Top of the World* and had a brief life until 11 April the same year. Three contestants competed, representing the USA, the UK and Australia. Each player played from their own country, via satellite. Even with Eamonn Andrews hosting the programme it was not the success it should have been. Eamonn got in a muddle with his questions and the technicalities involved were quite complicated. Just imagine holding a quiz over a telephone line with all the time delays involved when speaking to far away places. It not only confused Eamonn but the public as well. Dear old Eamonn got so flustered that when it got to the contestant who was answering questions on the life and music of Bob Dylan he asked, 'Why did Bob Dylan marry?'

'Why did Bob Dylan marry?' queried the contestant as the audience started to giggle.

Eamonn retorted, 'Yes, why did Bob Dylan marry ... no, no, I've got it wrong. *Who* did Bob Dylan marry?'

The eventual winner was James Eccleson, a 31-year-old insurance broker from Wirral, Merseyside who won a vintage 1924 Rolls-Royce (it makes a change from a washing machine). Although a second series was planned, it was never made. Eamonn was always protected from any bad news, and that was one thing that was coming in thick and fast about the show, especially from Australia. He thought it was going very well and being well received by the public until his make-up lady said how sorry she was to hear all the bad news about the show and he shouldn't let that worry him! Ooops!

Channel Four started broadcasting on 2 November 1982, and the first game show it broadcast was the word and maths game, *Countdown*. The show has been a continuing

Eamonn Andrews puts the questions in *Top of the World*.
James Eccleson, winner of *Top of the World*. © Thames TV

success to this day, but another commissioned by Channel Four had a very short life indeed. It was called *Jeopardy* and it was hoped it would be as successful here as it had been in the United States where it is still a top rating show. Our version lasted one series and achieved a rating of zero! The game is played by the presenter giving the answer and the contestants have to decide what the question is. For instance: I would say to you, 'It is 70 miles per hour' and you would say to me, 'What is the maximum road speed limit in this country?' Get the idea? Well, the show was a disaster here for the simple reason that the questions were too hard and consequently all the contestants had to be members of MENSA. That doesn't make for popular viewing. On one occasion there was a standby contestant who wasn't a member of MENSA but a very pleasant, reasonably bright, grandmother. A contestant didn't turn up so the grandmother substituted. As the game was so boring and not going too well a few easier questions were shuffled into the system. As luck would have it, the grandmother got through to the final round, and actually won the game by putting the correct question to the presenter's answer. What was the answer? It was 'Annie Walker'. And the question? 'She is the landlady of the Rovers Return'! MENSA eat your heart out.

Jeopardy was always seen as ITV's answer to *Mastermind* but alas it was not to be!

The ultimate personality quiz took to the air in 1985. Hosted by Cilla Black, *Blind Date* is one of the most successful game show formats on British television today and the beauty of it is that it is so simple. For those of you who have been on Mars for the past five years, the format is that Cilla introduces three single girls (or boys) who are all hoping for a blind date with an individual who is hidden from them. The girl or boy then asks questions which the hopeful partners answer in turn. From the responses the individual then takes his or her pick from the hidden three and off they go on their blind date. The date is filmed and played back into the show the next week and we, the viewers, see how they got on.

Cilla and three lovely fellas who want a *Blind Date*. © LWT

Since the show began it has become more and more stage managed. There is now a team of writers, and the responses appear to be scripted; indeed in most cases this is exactly what happens.

Being so popular, *Blind Date* is put under a microscope by the press and every month or so we are told by the tabloids that a married man has appeared or a contestant is divorced or some other scandal is revealed. But, no matter what happens, it is still one of the most popular game shows on television today.

Strike it Lucky first went on air on 29 October 1986. I have worked on it as researcher and associate producer for three years with my producer and good friend Maurice Leonard. We find the contestants, write most of the questions and programme the computers with the help of our team of technicians. It is a show that offers prizes in the form of household goods and holidays. The game reaches a climax with a jackpot game with possible winnings of £3,000. Over the years the host of the show, Michael Barrymore, has become a good friend and he really is the one responsible for the success of the show. Gradually it has moved from a straight game show to a combination of a comedy chat show and game show, a format which people enjoy as we regularly attract over 10 million viewers.

Naturally there are many other game shows that have been produced over the past forty years and I apologize for not including them all, but at least this brief history should have given you an insight into their development. Before we go any further it is interesting to note how much money can be won by appearing on TV.

The largest prize ever won on television wasn't on a game show but on a lottery. The *Guinness Book of Records* tells us on 24 July 1975 WABC–TV, New York City, transmitted the first televised Grand Tier draw of the State Lottery in which the winner took the grand prize of $1,000,000! Game shows don't have such rich pickings, but the money can build up. In the UK the biggest cash prize to date is £7,455 on *Winner Takes All* on 18 July 1986. This prize was won by computer expert Michael Dixon of Clwyd.

The prizes are there to be won and game shows will always require contestants. Everyone who applies stands a chance of appearing and winning. It is those who do not apply who stand no chance of appearing. After all, there are lots of prizes to be won. It's worth remembering that in years to come those prizes are going to get bigger and bigger!

Want to try? In these chapters you will be guided through the Crystal Maze of game shows and if you Play your Cards Right you could certainly Strike it Lucky and hit the Bullseye to Take your Pick of the game shows!

Read on . . .

Two

Why
Game Shows
are Made

Television is the growth industry of the 1990s and about 90 per cent of households in this country have a set. Over the past few years we have seen cable television become available in major towns and cities. If you walk down any street nowadays the chances are you will see a dish for receiving satellite services. But still the main stations received by all households are those known as terrestrial stations, i.e. BBC1, BBC2, ITV, Channel 4 and soon, Channel 5.

The BBC stations (including BBC radio) are funded directly by you, the viewer, paying your TV licence fees. The BBC has further income from selling the programmes they make to other television companies around the world via an associated company called BBC Enterprises. The BBC also makes money by selling merchandise associated with their programmes: T-shirts, books, videos, etc.

The independent television stations have no income from your television licence fee but make their money from selling advertising time around their programmes. Currently they are allowed to advertise for an average of seven minutes per hour. The ITV companies also make money, like the BBC, from selling the programmes they make around the world and selling associated merchandise. Both the BBC and ITV companies have further incomes from hiring out their facilities and staff talents to anyone who would like to make a television programme.

Essentially the satellite stations are exactly the same as ITV except the rules governing the amount of advertising and the programmes' standards will generally be more lax.

As all the above stations are transmitting at the same time to the same area there is great rivalry between the channels, and it can be seen that the station with the most popular programmes will gain the most viewers.

As more and more independent television stations come on air, the amount of money available for programme making goes down simply because the money from advertising has to go further. To attract more advertisers to a particular television station that station may put its advertising rates down but the end result is the same: less money all round. As there is less money coming in to a television company, they have less money to spend on programmes, which will mean the programme quality may go down. If this happens then the advertisers will cut their advertising because less people watch, and so the situation could become a vicious circle.

It has become apparent that the best way to make reasonable quality programmes for the least amount of money is to make many programmes of one type per studio day, thus utilizing the expensive television facilities to the maximum. Really, the only types of programme that lend themselves to this formula are simple chat shows and game shows. And which is the more popular with viewers? THE GAME SHOW!

So now that it is far cheaper for a television company to make game shows they will want to make sure that theirs is better than a rival's, and that is where you come in! Of course it goes without saying that the game itself has

BRITISH TOP 100

© Broadcast magazine

		Channel	Day	Millions	
1	(2) Coronation Street	ITV	W,Sa	16.1	(13.5/2.6)
2	(1) Coronation Street	ITV	F,Sa	15.5	(12.3/3.2)
3	(3) Coronation Street	ITV	M,W	15.0	(13.9/1.1)
4	(5) Neighbours	BBC1	M-F	14.0	(4.8/9.2)
5	(6) EastEnders	BBC1	Tu,Su	13.6	(10.8/2.8)
6	(4) EastEnders	BBC1	Th,Su	13.5	(10.3/3.2)
7	(7) Strike It Lucky	ITV	M	10.4	
8	(—) Eurovision Song Contest	BBC1	Sa	10.2	
9	(11) Home And Away	ITV	M-F	9.7	(2.9/6.8)
10	(—) Mistress Of Suspense	ITV	W	9.5	
11	(10) Emmerdale	ITV	Tu	9.5	
12	(15) The Bill	ITV	Tu	9.4	
13	(37) News, Sport And Weather	BBC1	Sa	9.3	
14	(8) The Bill	ITV	Th	9.2	
15	(31) Bangkok Hilton	BBC1	F	9.0	
16	(18) Joint Account	BBC1	M	8.9	
17	(—) Ronn Lucas Show	ITV	W	8.9	
18	(17) A Question Of Sport	BBC1	Tu	8.9	
19	(44) That's Life	BBC1	Su	8.5	
20	(12) Through The Keyhole	ITV	F	8.4	
21	(75) News And Weather	BBC1	Su	8.4	
22	(9) Birds Of A Feather	BBC1	Th	8.3	
23	(14) Just For Laughs	ITV	M	8.1	
24	(—) Up The Garden Path	ITV	W	8.1	
25	(20) Surgical Spirits	ITV	F	8.1	
26	(47) Jeeves And Wooster	ITV	Su	8.0	
27	(58) Perfect Scoundrels	ITV	Su	8.0	
28	(19) Emmerdale	ITV	Th	8.0	
29	(13) Busman's Holiday	ITV	W	7.9	
30	(22) To The Manor Born	BBC1	Tu	7.9	
31	(33) The Chief	ITV	F	7.6	
32	(—) Upper Hand	ITV	Tu	7.4	
33	(53) The Black Adder	BBC1	Su	7.3	
34	(74) Mastermind	BBC1	Su	7.3	
35	(50) World In Action	ITV	M	7.2	
36	(30) Baywatch	ITV	Sa	7.1	
37	(21) The Two Of Us	ITV	Sa	7.0	
38	(48) News At Ten	ITV	M-F	6.9	
39	(46) Chancer	ITV	Tu	6.7	
40	(40) Nine O'Clock News	BBC1	M-F	6.7	
41	(28) Brian Conley — This Way Up	ITV	F	6.7	
42	(—) Assault On Precinct 13	BBC2	Su	6.7	
43	(51) News	ITV	Su	6.6	
44	(67) News	ITV	Sa	6.6	
45	(35) Six O'Clock News	BBC1	M-F	6.6	
46	(25) Davro	ITV	Sa	6.5	
47	(—) Cassidy	BBC1	Tu	6.4	
48	(—) 13 At Dinner	ITV	M	6.3	
49	(39) Paradise	BBC1	F	6.0	
50	(57) All Creatures Great And Small	BBC1	Su	6.0	

Source: BARB

Satellite TV goes to Davro's head at No 46.

Sheila Hancock dreams on in Single Voices at No 90.

Programmes with split networking may be under-represented in these ratings.

Source: BARB

		Channel	Day	Millions
51	(45) Tomorrow's World — 25th Birthday	BBC1	Th	5.7
52	(52) Dallas	BBC1	W	5.7
53	(43) Top Of The Pops	BBC1	Th	5.6
54	(—) Meteor	BBC1	Sa	5.6
55	(—) Letting Go	ITV	Sa	5.3
56	(54) Aspel And Company	ITV	Sa	5.2
57	(49) 'Allo 'Allo	BBC1	F	5.2
58	(98) This Week	ITV	Th	4.9
59	(72) Wogan	BBC1	M,W,F	4.7
60	(66) Highway	ITV	Su	4.7
61	(55) The Flying Doctors	BBC1	Sa	4.6
62	(60) Steal	ITV	Sa	4.6
63	(71) TECX	ITV	Th	4.5
64	(76) News At 5.40	ITV	M-F	4.5
65	(64) Style Trial	BBC1	Tu	4.5
66	(73) A Kind Of Living	ITV	Su	4.4
67	(61) Not With A Bang	ITV	Su	4.4
68	(—) Lennon	ITV	Sa	4.3
69	(—) Miami Vice	BBC1	M	4.3
70	(—) Murder In Coweta County	BBC2	M	4.2
71	(70) Blockbusters	ITV	Tu,Th	4.1
72	(32) Inside Story	BBC1	W	4.0
73	(86) In Sickness And In Health	BBC1	M	4.0
74	(79) The Clothes Show	BBC1	Su	4.0
75	(90) Bullseye	ITV	Su	4.0
76	(—) Praise Be	BBC1	Su	3.9
77	(—) Battle Of The River Plate	BBC1	Su	3.9
78	(78) Blue Peter	BBC1	M,Th	3.9
79	(—) The Crystal Maze	C4	Th	3.8
80	(87) The Gift	BBC1	W	3.7
81	(77) Brookside	C4	W,Sa	3.7 (2.4/1.3)
82	(84) Brookside	C4	M,Sa	3.7 (2.6/1.2)
83	(95) Paramount City	BBC1	Sa	3.6
84	(—) Panorama	BBC1	M	3.5
85	(—) Lowdown	BBC1	W	3.4
86	(91) Kon Tiki Man	BBC1	W	3.4
87	(—) Brave New Wilderness	ITV	Su	3.3
88	(83) Sporting Triangles	ITV	Th	3.3
89	(93) One O'Clock News	BBC1	M-F	3.2
90	(—) Single Voices	BBC1	Su	3.2
91	(—) M*A*S*H	BBC2	W	3.1
92	(—) On The Black Hill	C4	Th	3.1
93	(—) Midweek Sports Special	ITV	W	3.1
94	(—) Best Of British	BBC1	M	3.1
95	(—) Roseanne	C4	F	3.1
96	(—) First Tuesday	ITV	Tu	3.0
97	(—) Cheers	C4	F	3.0
98	(99) Round The Twist	BBC1	F	3.0
99	(—) Teenage Mutant Hero Turtles	BBC1	Tu	3.0
100	(89) Results	ITV	Sa	3.0

to be good and has to have the right host, but providing that those criteria are met then the success of the show will also depend on the contestants the show uses. With success comes good ratings, and ratings are all-important in television. Every show that is transmitted will get a rating to indicate how many people watched it.

There are many ways of discovering how many people watched a programme. You could simply walk down your street and ask ten people. From those ten people you could work out a 'top ten', but the *sample* would be very small and not a broad representation of the viewing public. The professional way is a little more complicated but far more accurate.

In this country, the Broadcasters Audience Research Board (BARB) commission a company called Audits for Great Britain (AGB) to provide the ratings. AGB have 3,030 television sets in homes across the country which have a meter attached to them. These meters are connected to a central computer which can tell which programmes are being watched at any one time. These homes are known as panel homes in the business, and the 3,030 sample is carefully selected to be as fair a representation of the viewing public as possible. (The number of panel homes is soon to be increased to 4,500 to make the ratings system even more representative.) To choose their sample AGB travel around the country interviewing householders who may be possible panel viewers. Essentially, the sample has to be as broad as possible and include the whole range of socioeconomic groups and age ranges. The interviewers also take into account the number of televisions in the house and the average number of hours per week the members of the household watch.

The beauty of the AGB computer system is that the sample is nationwide and as the sample viewers can be categorized into age groups and social groups a very accurate breakdown of the viewing public can be achieved.

This will be of great benefit to programme planners and advertisers. For example, it would be quite pointless advertising make-up during a programme aimed at a majority audience of male viewers. Similarly it would be pointless to advertise Rolls-Royce cars during a show which attracts an audience that couldn't afford to buy one.

After one week's viewing a very important ratings chart is produced, using the figures provided by AGB. All the ratings are collated into the British Top 100. It is from this chart that the top ten programmes are discovered. You may have the list published in your national paper. It is from the top 100 that the performance of any one show can be seen against all the other programmes for that week. The full chart is published every week in the television trade press, the main weekly trade magazine for television being *Broadcast*. So ratings are important and because of this, you, the contestant, will be very important to any game show.

Why, I hear you ask, is the BBC bothered about ratings? After all, they don't have to sell advertising time and their income remains the same whatever they transmit. This very point has fascinated me for some time and I put it to John Bishop, the assistant head of variety at the BBC. He told me that the ratings act as a guide for them. Admittedly it is not as dreadful for the BBC if a programme falls in the ratings as for ITV. If an ITV programme falls then the amount that can be realistically charged for advertising time around that particular show will fall. John Bishop pointed out with a wry smile, 'Psychologically it's good if you can beat the opposition, and you can see if you've done so from the ratings chart. But it is important to make sure you have a good product when the game show hits the air. Ratings can tell you this.' With this in mind I asked him what does make a good game show, and he told me:

1. The show must be entertaining
2. It has to be intellectually stimulating and intelligent enough to sustain viewers
3. It must contain an element of skill
4. The host is of prime importance
5. Without contestants there's no show. They are second only to the host. Contestants need to be fun, extrovert and intelligent.

To make sure the show works and there are no gremlins in the format, the BBC 'dry run' their shows for some considerable time. A dry run is simply when a show is staged but not shown to the public. For example, John Bishop told me that the most successful recent game show from the BBC was *Bob's Full House* hosted by Bob Monkhouse. There were eighteen months of dry runs before it was made properly and shown on BBC1. Similarly, *Takeover Bid*, hosted by Bruce Forsyth, had twelve months of dry runs. These runs are normally held in rehearsal rooms, without any cameras and with dummy contestants, usually actors. Shows then usually go into the studio for a 'pilot' to be made. This is a recording that is made just as it is intended, with an audience and real contestants, but it will not normally be transmitted. Again this is to see if the logistics and technicalities all work and will come together 'on the night'. ('On the night' simply means the actual time when the show is recorded or transmitted live).

The fact is that a lot of work goes into the simplest of shows to make sure it works and will be entertaining. When you apply for a show, go for an audition or even appear, make sure you too have done some work to prepare yourself; it is only fair to the TV team, and it's also the only surefire way to succeed.

Three

Which Show

to Apply

For

Most television companies make game shows of one sort or another. There are fifteen main ITV companies as well as Channel 4, BBC1, BBC2, the satellite channels and soon Channel 5.

Other companies may be commissioned by the main television stations to make game shows for them. These are known as independent companies, simply because they are independent of the television station that will be broadcasting their show. There are scores of independent companies making television programmes; for instance, Celador Productions make the game show *Everybody's Equal* for Thames Television and Regent Productions make *Fifteen to One* for Channel Four. Come 1992, the government has stated, 25 per cent of all the programmes broadcast by television stations have to be made by independent companies. So there will be more independent companies making game shows which, added to the existing broadcast companies also making them, means that your talents as a good contestant will be in great demand!

Different types of shows require different types of contestants. For the purpose of this book a subtle distinction to make at this stage is the difference between a quiz show and a game show. Two good examples of a quiz show are *Fifteen to One* and – the Rolls-Royce of them all – *Mastermind*. In a quiz show, knowledge is all

William G. Stewart, questionmaster of *Fifteen to One*. © Regent Productions

important ... specialized and general knowledge with *Mastermind* and a broad general knowledge with *Fifteen to One*. The personality of the contestant is of no consequence just as long as he or she can answer the questions.

With game shows things are a little different. The personality of the contestants is a major factor directly related to the show's success. For example, a brilliant

Mastermind contestant would not necessarily be a good contestant on Michael Barrymore's *Strike it Lucky*. With *Strike it Lucky* the personality of the contestants is very important along with them being reasonably good at general knowledge. Another example would be *Play Your Cards Right*. Bruce Forsyth had to have a rapport with the couples playing the game. The general knowledge element required to play the game was minimal as the show was based on luck and thrived on the personality of Bruce Forsyth and that of the contestants.

The professionals have their own definitions. Jeremy Beadle tells us, 'The difference between a game show and a quiz is simple. In game shows you stand up. Once you understand that colossal subtlety, you can disguise a simple quiz show as a complicated game show.' However, Anthony Gruner, chief executive of Talbot Television, says that 'The quiz show is one-dimensional, like a one-act play. The game show always has its climax, the end game. It's a three-act play, and the studio audience is the Greek chorus.'

Another important distinction to make is the difference between reward shows and non-reward shows.

For example on the quiz show, *Fifteen to One*, the winner receives a replica of a 4th-century head of Buddah while a Waterford crystal cut-glass bowl is the winner's trophy with *Mastermind*. On game shows there are prizes galore to be had! For instance, on *Family Fortunes*, contestants can win clothes, household goods and up to £3,000 cash.

There is one other group that should be mentioned. For example, shows like *Countdown*, *What's My Line?* and *Blind Date*, which have minimal reward and rely on a specific skill or oddity of the contestant taking part. With *Countdown* the contestant has to be an instant lexicographer (look it up!) and mathematician. Contestants taking part in *What's My Line?* do so because gen erally they have a strange occupation, and the basic requirement for anyone to appear on *Blind Date* is that they should be good looking, fun, able to remember the lines written for them and then tell all to the Sunday papers after their particular programme has gone out! Rewards on these shows are again, minimal ... a set of dictionaries if you win *Countdown*, a certificate if you beat the panel at *What's My Line?* or a day trip to somewhere you didn't want to go to with someone you didn't want to go with for *Blind Date*. However, it's all fun and that is what game shows are all about. Incidentally, on the United States version of *What's My Line?* for every 'no' answer the contestant used to get $5, so after ten no's he could come away with $50 making it, in true American style, a reward show!

Most people probably already know which show they would like to appear on but the question is, would they be the right type in the eyes of the producer? If you have selected your programme, stand back and compare yourself to those contestants already taking part in it. Would you fit? Why were they chosen? What makes them different?

Bruce Forsyth, telling me what he looks for in contestants for *The Generation Game*, said they have to be 'outgoing, physically fit, bright, have a good sense of humour, and have the ability to laugh at themselves ... and at my jokes!' Paul Daniels laid down the ground rules for picking contestants for his show, *Every Second Counts*. He told me, 'The ideal contestants for the show are married couples over 25 years old and under 40, as the under 25s are either painfully shy or horrendous looking, while the over 40s develop a fear of being shown up.' I did say to him that those were very rather generalized comments and he did qualify his statement by adding, 'There are exceptions.'

If you are unsure which show you would like to apply

for, the first thing to do is decide which type of show you would be good at. Check the following points:

1. Which type of show would you like to appear on – a quiz show or a game show?
2. Do you want to make money from your appearance? i.e., a reward or non-reward show?
3. Do you have an outgoing personality?
4. Are you good at general knowledge?
5. Do you have a strong specialized subject you could answer questions on?
6. Do you have any family or friends who could join you on the programme as partners?

Having done that, you should now be able to decide which specific show you would be good at by comparing your assets to those of the contestants you see on the screen. Now spend a few weeks watching as many game shows as you possibly can and decide which you would be good at.

Having decided on your goal, you have to try to get on the show you've picked.

To get on to a game show you have to apply to the company concerned for an application form, which you fill in and return. Then you will (hopefully) be invited to an audition which you will (hopefully) pass. You will then be short-listed for the show. Finally the day comes when you go on to the show, win lots of money or other prizes and then go home to celebrate your winnings and new-found and short-lived fame!

It sounds easy doesn't it? The fact is for every game show there are literally thousands of applicants and only a few get through to play the game. For instance, with *Strike it Lucky* we audition about 3,000 hopeful couples for just sixty places. It goes without saying that a show that uses more contestants in a series will audition more hopeful participants. A show that uses fifteen contestants per programme is *Fifteen to One*. William G. Stewart, its producer and host, told me that he auditions some 5,000 applicants per year and over the three years the show has been on the air 6,000 contestants have been used! William was very keen to point out to me that 99 per cent of all applicants get auditions and all auditionees hear how they did within two weeks.

One word of advice here is that if you intend to apply for a show which requires you to have good general knowledge then you could do yourself no harm by joining a quiz league. Many pubs run quiz leagues and you don't have to be a serious boozer to join them. These leagues are becoming very popular, proven by the fact that they have their own show on ITV called *Quiz Night*. It will also be good practice as you will learn how to formulate answers in your head and *speak* the answers to questions. That is not as easy as it looks especially if it is a timed round and you have to think quickly.

Television producers get literally hundreds of requests from would-be contestants every week. What they look for is someone who will be of benefit to their programme. Remember, the success of most game shows depends upon the format of the game, the personality of the host and the personalities of the contestants . . . that is why you are important!

Four

The Route to Appearing on a Game Show

To recap, this is the normal route taken by contestants who appear on game shows:

Decide which show
Write to show requesting an application form
Fill in and return the application form
Wait
Invited to audition
Pass audition
Invited onto show

It looks easy, doesn't it, but as I have said there are many pitfalls along the way. Remember, before you apply for anything: look at your good points and decide which show is going to be best for you. Obviously, if you are no good at general knowledge, don't apply for a show that has a strong general knowledge content. If you have a good specialist knowledge then see if there is a show that can accommodate your talents. For instance, you may be very good at identifying music; if that's the case then apply for a show like *Key Notes*. If you know everything there is to know about television shows then *Telly Addicts* will be the one for you. Stand back and decide what type of personality you have. Are you really an extrovert? Remember on many shows you have to shine and be bubbly, but there are others where personality isn't too important.

Don't waste your time, and other people's, by fooling yourself and applying for the wrong show. You know yourself better than anyone else possibly can, and you will know which show you would be best on, so go for that!

Now, where do you apply? In Appendix One at the back of this book there is a comprehensive list of quiz and game shows. Alongside each is the name of the company who makes it. That is the company to apply to, and Appendix Two gives a comprehensive list of those companies' addresses. Find the company you want and get writing! Also you will discover that many television companies will advertise for contestants both on TV and in the press. Keep your ears and eyes open!

Action Time is an independent game show production company and they have a full-time contestant research unit. They find all the contestants for Scottish Television and Yorkshire Television and that includes shows that are not even Action Time productions. They recently found the contestants for the series of *Pyramid Game* that Television South produced, as well as for *Wife of the Week* which Yorkshire TV, who own the rights, are making for satellite broadcasting. Action Time advertise massively for contestants in the press and also on tele-vision. Returned application forms are filed under fifteen different cities and sub-divided into male and female. When the producer of a game show knows what type of contestant he is looking for he simply sifts through the files for suitable-looking contestants and organizes interviews to pick his contestants.

In November 1990 BBC Television advertised in the national press for contestants to appear on their game shows. The advert read: 'Stardom on BBC Television . . . Applications are invited for contestants on Paul Daniels' *Every Second Counts* (married couples), Bruce Forsyth's *Generation Game* (related couples), Bruce Forsyth's *Takeover Bid* (bright singles), *Big Break* (snooker format general knowledge quiz – ability to play not essential)'. The advert continued, 'If you are fun loving, outgoing and would like to be a TV star, then write with an SAE to . . .'

All the responses went to one room at the BBC Television Centre. When I spoke to the three girls and one chap who collated them they said that for the *Generation Game* they had sent out 20,000 application forms, while the other shows in the advertisement were all level-pegging at about 10,000 applications apiece!

Many TV companies will have their own systems of advertising for, selecting and interviewing contestants. If you are applying to an individual company, there is one word of advice. Avoid writing asking to apply for 'any game shows you have vacancies on'. That will immediately prove that you don't care what show you go on and you haven't put any thought into your initial application. Apply for a specific show; unless, of course, you have seen a company advertising for contestants where individual shows were not specified.

Having decided which show you want to apply for *write* for an application form to the appropriate company. If you telephone for a form they may simply ask you to write in anyway. I would suggest that you enclose a large stamped addressed envelope, whether it is asked for or not. This will ensure that a form can be sent back to you straight away rather than having to wait for someone to type an envelope. Remember that producers get thousands of applications every week and if you make their job easier you will be one step ahead of the rest.

All mainstream game shows will have a form to fill in

so there is little point in going into great detail in your initial letter. Be straightforward and to the point. Here is a suggestion as to how you would write that initial letter:

The Contestant Researcher,
XYZ Game,
ABC Television,
Television Centre,
123 Television Road,
Weatherfield,
Lancs
WL90 9DG

Dear Sir,

RE: XYZ GAME

I wish to apply to be a contestant on the XYZ
Game.
    I would be grateful if you would send me the
appropriate application form.
    For your convenience I have enclosed a stamped
addressed envelope.

    Yours faithfully,
    John Smith

I would suggest that you do not address your letter directly to the producer of the programme – unless, of course, you have seen an advertisement so to do – for his secretary may well pass his mail unopened to him directly, and it is not normally he who sends out application forms. He is too busy producing shows to get involved in secretarial duties, and will only come into the picture when he is organizing auditions after his staff have sifted through the thousands of applications returned to the office. When I have been busy I have found it quite frustrating to find a stack of mail addressed directly to me, some marked 'Personal', only to discover that they are from people wanting application forms for a show I am involved with. One producer I know has been known to file such letters directly into the rubbish bin, especially if the letter itself starts with 'Dear . . .' then his Christian name! So beware!

A good tip here is to photocopy all your correspondence and keep the copies safely so you know exactly what you have sent to which programme. If, over a period, you apply for more than one show this will prove invaluable for it may be months before you are contacted.

To give you some idea of the waiting time involved I can cite two examples from shows I have been involved with. In 1990 I had between thirty and fifty people a day writing to *Strike it Lucky* applying to be contestants. This mounted up to thousands of *unsolicited* applications over the year. We always try to audition as many applicants as possible, but it is not hard to imagine that it could be up to a year before an applicant is invited to an audition. I am also involved in *What's My Line?* and because there are so many excellent odd occupations in existence some people I have seen recently applied up to three years ago for a place on the programme. So you can see you may have to be patient.

Five

The

Application

Form

So now you have requested an application form to appear as a contestant on a show. It must be emphasized again that television companies get literally thousands of such requests so there may be a wait before you receive one, while if you have written to a show not currently in production all applications will be put on 'hold' until it starts up again.

There is no such thing as a standard application form for a game show. Each television company has different ones. Some forms will be quite comprehensive while others will be fairly simple. At the end of this section there is a typical example. You must remember that the purpose of filling in an application form is for you to get chosen to audition to appear on the programme, so the form will become your shop window. It is through the form that you have to sell yourself, so follow a few simple rules:

1. Make sure you know which show you are applying for! (It does sound obvious, but recently I had a lady applying for *Strike it Lucky* who said that she was looking forward to

meeting Paul Daniels . . . she thought she was
applying for *Every Second Counts!*)
2. Before you start filling in the form, study it
carefully
3. Make sure you know which sections to fill in
with what information
4. Follow any instructions on the form to the letter
5. Make sure your writing is legible. If it says use
black pen don't use blue! If the form doesn't
specify anything and your handwriting isn't
very good, type the form or get someone to type
it for you.

Now that's the basic rules over and done with, what about the
content of the form itself? You will be asked some standard
questions like name, age and address. When you fill in your
age don't put 'over 21'. The question is there because the
producers need to know how old you are. If you are shy
about your age then don't even apply to go on television!

For shows where your personality is going to be very
important, when you fill in the form think about the
presenter talking to you. What will he talk to you about?
If there are a few titbits you can include on the form, do so.
Have you an odd name! Maybe it's your middle name? You
can even try putting your nickname on the form if there is
a good story about it that you could relay to the presenter.
What about your address? Maybe you live at 9 The Street,
Manchester, but has the house got a name? If it has, put
that down as well, especially if it is an odd one. Never feel
embarrassed about living at Wookey Hole or Knotty Ash
or anywhere with a strange name. It could all be useful
material for the programme, but *do not make things up* or
'go over the top' and be silly.

Many forms will ask about hobbies and interests. If you
have an unusual hobby, make sure you put it down. Again,
imagine that the presenter is interviewing you on the
programme. What is he going to chat to you about? If
you have a quirky hobby or interest then this will be an

added bonus. In my experience hundreds of well-meaning applicants put down 'Watching people', 'Meeting people' and 'Sleeping'. We all watch people and we meet people every day and we all sleep, so don't put them down as a hobby because they're not, they're what we all do!

If you like travelling then put that down, but not if the only travel you did was a couple of years ago when you went on holiday to the Costa del Sol! But there again if there is a good story about that particular trip try putting it down as it could be a talking point. If you put down that you like reading make sure you know who you like reading because you'll get asked! I asked one lady during some recent auditions, 'I see you like reading – who wrote *Hollywood Wives*?'

The lady said, 'Jilly Cooper.'

'No, it wasn't her,' I said, 'but do you like reading Jilly's books?'

'Oh yes, she is my favourite,' she said.

'OK,' I said, 'who wrote the best seller called *Riders*?'

'Oh no, I don't know who wrote that one!' replied the bookworm.

On many forms you will be asked what newspapers you read and what television programmes you watch. Don't lie! This information will be important when selecting possible contestants for audition, for many shows demand a wide mix of people with different interests and backgrounds.

Some forms may contain some general knowledge questions. If they do, make sure you answer them correctly. Remember that as you have the questions all you have to do is go to the library and look up the answers if you don't know them. However, on some application forms they say do not use reference books. The application form that Action Time sends out has forty difficult general knowledge questions that you are asked to answer and they state, 'Do not use reference books'. I was particularly fascinated by that, so I went along to Manchester to speak to the managing director of Action Time, Stephen Leahy, to ask him about the form that his company sends out.

'The questions are there to frighten the contestants,' said Stephen. 'If people go to the library to find out the answers then that is fine. It shows they have initiative. If a form is returned with none of the questions answered correctly, it is normally filed in the rubbish bin!'

However, initiative apart, if you are hopeless at general knowledge then do not apply for a show which requires contestants who are good at answering general knowledge questions. If you have limited general knowledge and you have bluffed your way through the whole application form, you will be found out if you are invited to an audition!

Even more formidable than the Action Time form is the one which is sent out for *The Krypton Factor*. Gail Watkins, the contestant co-ordinator from Granada Television, told me that the form usually runs to seven or eight pages, and last year 10,000 were sent out. Many of the same individuals apply year after year, so the form is changed annually as it contains a series of mental agility and general knowledge tests. One very important section consists of questions on the health of the applicant. Obviously, with the physical assault course element of the programme it would be absolutely foolish to do anything but tell the truth in this section. That part of the game is most strenuous and physically exhausting.

It has to be said at this stage that many shows don't want contestants with great general knowledge and mental agility along with the physique of Frank Bruno! There are those that look for people with personality and wit. It has to be remembered that some of the general knowledge questions on some forms the normal man in the street wouldn't know anyway . . . in some cases it is all a test to see how you fill in the form, if indeed you can be bothered to do so having seen it. It is a filtering process. Action Time put a clever little piece on their form: 'What 3 adjectives describe you most accurately?' If you receive an application form which contains this question, or something similar, then think very carefully before putting pen to paper. As Stephen Leahy says,

> 'You get people who put "effervescent, witty and bright", and when they come and see us they are the dullest people you have ever met in your life! If that is the genuine perception of themselves then we can challenge them on it at the audition. If people put "dull, boring and stupid" on the form then either they have a wonderful sense of humour or they're telling the truth.'

Whatever the case, laziness will not get you an audition so spend time on the application . . . it could be the key to thousands of pounds! Never be frightened by a form that you receive. Always fill it in. If you don't you will never get an audition for a show!

A golden rule is: don't lie on the form because the producers will catch you out! Really, the bottom line is that that form is your shop window; if you have dressed it properly you will have sold yourself and you will be successful in getting an audition.

Many shows will ask you to send in a photograph of yourself with the form. Again, remember that we are dealing with television here, not radio! Make yourself look your best.

I would suggest that the type of photograph you send will depend upon the show you are applying for. If it is one with a comedy or fun element then send a photograph which not only shows you enjoying yourself, but also stands out from the crowd. Don't send obscene photographs, but don't send boring ones either. Wear something smart and make sure your hair is tidy. Basically look your best, in fact just as you would if you were about to go on to the programme itself! If the form doesn't specify a size of photograph them remember that nowadays you can get twenty-four photographs developed for about £2. If you haven't got a camera then get a friend who has to take some decent photographs of you. Remember, the photograph is an opportunity for you to express yourself visually and you can show your sense of humour here as well. It is really up to you.

Here are some guidelines for your photographs:

1. Remember you are the subject, not the background, so don't make the background the focus of attention. Many photographs I have seen attached to application forms have a central heating radiator as a background. Radiators are not photogenic!

2. Avoid standing in front of a mirror or glass when shooting with a flash as this will cause a very bad reflective flash on the photograph

3. Make sure that only the people who are applying for the show appear on the photograph. More will only confuse the producer, but if you are applying for a show like *Family Fortunes* or *Telly Addicts* then all the family who are going on the show need to be on that photograph

4. Look your best. It's television, not radio!

5. What will make your photograph different? Think about it. Remember it is every man for himself when it comes to getting onto game shows.

With your photograph, anything to make you stand out helps as it may make the producer remember you. Think about this very carefully and try to relate the photograph to the show you are applying for. For instance, if you had to send in a photo with your application for *Telly Addicts*, how about lining up the family who are applying on a sofa as if watching the TV, say one with a *TV Times*, one with a *Radio Times*, one with a remote control and the last member of the team eating TV supper off his or her lap. This would show you have thought about the photograph and have related it to the show. Whatever you do, remember we need to see the faces of the possible contestants!

Another example would be a possible group photograph for *Busman's Holiday*. Why not have all three contenders posed by, on or in a bus and dressed in whatever their work clothes would be. For *The Krypton Factor*, the contestant could be posed on an assault course, perhaps hanging from a rope. Think about it and the ideas will come flooding to you.

The photograph you send can also help the producers see that you are physically fit, especially if you are getting on in years, if that is a requirement of the show to which you are applying. Most shows consider that the photograph is a very important part of the application so make it the best possible. I have been told that some busy shows may select contestants for auditions mainly from the photographs.

Having completed the application form, spend 10p or so photocopying it. Some time may elapse before you hear from the television company, and it is essential that you can remind yourself what you wrote on it when you are called for an interview. Check the form again before you send it back. Have you filled in all the correct sections? Have you answered all the general knowledge questions on the form (if there are any) to the best of your ability? Is there anything you have missed?

One useful tip here. Programme companies file thousands of application forms. It is a great help if you can return yours unfolded, in a large stiff-backed envelope. This will help with your presentation (rather than them having a screwed-up piece of paper to file!) and it will also help keep your photographs uncreased.

One last thing before you send it all off. Does the form say send a stamped addressed envelope? If so, it is very important that you do. If it doesn't, then send one anyway. It will show you care about your application. Now pop the form, stamped addressed envelope and your photograph(s) into an envelope and send them back to the television company . . . and keep your fingers crossed!

Ref No.

**Please attach
a <u>non-returnable</u>
photograph
here**

ACTION TIME

CONTESTANT
APPLICATION FORM

Name:	
Address:	
Daytime Telephone No:	
Home Telephone No. (If different):	
Date of Birth:	Day: Month: Year:
Occupation:	
Marital Status:	
Details of any previous TV quiz show appearances:	
Are you in any Quiz Leagues? If so detail:	
Hobbies:	1.
	2.
	3.
	4.
Which National Newspaper do you read?:	
What are your local newspapers:	
In which of the following cities would you prefer to be interviewed – Aberdeen, Belfast, Birmingham, Bristol, Cambridge, Cardiff, Edinburgh, Glasgow, Leeds, London, Manchester, Newcastle or Southampton.	

Please complete the following 40 General Knowledge questions. We recommend that you complete this form in one sitting in a quiet room away from all distractions, and don't worry if you can't complete all the questions – some of them are deliberately tough! Do not use reference books – you won't be able to use them if you qualify for the General Knowledge Test later on.

1. Upon whose life was the TV drama "Across The Lake" based?

2. Which Middle Eastern country's flag shows a Cedar tree?

3. Who designed the Royal Albert Bridge at Saltash which forms the rail link between Devon and Cornwall?

4. What new kind of food called "Pom" was sold for the first time in Britain in 1946?

5. Which Trades Union was expelled from the T.U.C. at this year's Annual Conference?

6. What's the first name of Princess Annes' daughter?

7. Which city gave its name to a three-coloured ice-cream of chocolate, vanilla and strawberry flavours?

8. In Shakespeare's "Hamlet", what is the name of the Prince of Denmark's mother?

9. What do divers call decompression sickness caused by bubbles of nitrogen in the blood?

10. Which Lisbon football club was twice winner of the European Cup in its early days?

11. February 1962 saw the publication of Britain's first colour supplement – to which newspaper did it belong?

12. Baroness Maria Von Trapp's life story was the inspiration for which musical?

13. For what famous forgery crime was Konrad Kujau brought to trial in 1984?

14. To which country did California belong until 1848?

15. Until the 19th Century, Shoguns were the ruling class in which country?

16. In road transport, the letters H.G.V. stand for what?

17. Which country became an Independent Republic outside the Commonwealth in January 1948?

18. From which common British tree do conkers come?

19. Sugar and ground what, are the main ingredients of marzipan?

20. What is Royal Crown Derby?

21. Which village in Cambridgeshire has a reputation for a cheese it never produced?

22. What is the name of the ninth month of the Muslim Calendar set aside for fasting?

23. Who is the presenter of the ITV quiz "The Krypton Factor"?

24. Who judged the beauty contest between Athena, Aphrodite and Hera that led to the Trojan war?

25. What is the surname of Leonid Brezhnev's son-in-law who was charged with corruption in September 1988?

26. Which lies north of the Equator – The Tropic of Cancer or The Tropic of Capricorn?

27. Tirana is the Capital of which Eastern European country?

28. In pre-decimal money, if you subtracted a Crown from a Guinea, how much would you have left?

29. What's the British equivalent of the "Nightstick" used by an American policeman?

30. Who became President of the USSR in 1985?

31. "For Valour" is the simple inscription on which award?

32. Which distinguished actor won an Oscar for his role as butler to a drunken Dudley Moore in the film "Arthur"?

33. Which famous lexicographer married Mrs Elizabeth Porter in Derby in 1735?

34. The former Portuguese colony of Goa is now part of which country?

35. Who solved the Riddle of the Sphinx?

36. The winner of the 1907 Nobel Prize for Literature died in 1936. He is rumoured to be a favourite writer of Mrs Thatcher. Name him.

37. Name the Minister of Defence who resigned from the cabinet in the wake of the Westland affair.

38. Black Down is the highest point of which range of hills?

39. In which Olympic sport do competitors in races stop at the finish line and not pass it?

40. In which English city did Roger Bannister run the first sub-four minute mile on May 6th 1954?

Thank you for completing your Contestant Application Form. We are looking for lively, cheerful people with good general knowledge.
Our Contestants will need to be quick-witted, fast on the buzzer and not be shy about appearing on television.

If your initial application is successful, you will be invited to one of a number of centres throughout the UK for an interview. After completing your application form, it will be placed on file until we are making a suitable quiz. You will not hear from us until that time.

What are your favourite quizzes?:

What 3 adjectives describe you most accurately?:

What has been your most interesting experience (in not more than 40 words):

Please return this application to: Contestant Applications,
                                    Action Time Ltd.,
                                    PO Box 121,
                                    Manchester M60 1EX

to arrive as soon as possible for priority consideration.

Action Time is the leading Independent Television Production Company specialising in the production of Quiz and Game Shows for ITV and BBC and other networks throughout the world.

Six

The

Audition

Why are auditions held? Simply in order that the producers or contestant researchers can see if you will be of benefit to their programme. After all, you have filled in the application form in hope of getting an audition. If you are successful then you have passed stage one; now the producers will want to see what you look like, hear what you sound like, discover what knowledge you have of your specialist subject and/or general knowledge, and they will want to discover what your personality is like. So what do you do when one morning you are sitting at the breakfast table opening your mail and you discover that in your hand is your invitation to an audition for the game show you have applied for?

The first rule is: DON'T PANIC!

If you have applied for more than one show make sure you know which one you will be auditioning for. This is where your photo-copied application form will come in handy. Find the copy of your form and read it *carefully*.

Now re-read the letter and check the location, date and time of your audition. Will you be able to attend? Most companies should let you know about auditions about three weeks before they happen. In the letter you may be asked to telephone their office to make sure you can attend. Check all the details and then contact the office to confirm your audition. While you are on the telephone double check the date, location and time.

Auditions are normally held in hotels all over the country. The production team may see literally hundreds of possible contestants for only a few places, but feel proud that you have got through this first stage, as you will be one of the lucky ones.

Finally the day has come for the audition.

Really there is no getting away from the fact that it will be like going for a job interview and you will be nervous. If you are terribly nervous in front of the two or three interviewers then what will you be like in front of a studio audience being chatted to by the presenter with half a dozen cameras pointing at you?!

The second audition rule, then, is: ENJOY YOURSELF. But be careful not to be flippant.

A major point to remember at an audition is that the show is the production team's life. Television people are an odd breed in that they enjoy their work and more often than not business and pleasure are intertwined. They eat, sleep and breathe the programme. When they go home at night after working at the studio they often carry on working by reading and modifying scripts and dreaming up new ideas and ways of improving the programme. Television people are egomaniacs. Whatever you do, never dent the ego of a television person. It doesn't matter what role they play in the set-up, they are all as bad as each other. If you talk to a cameraman remember that he will be the best cameraman you will ever meet; if you meet a sound man he will produce the best sound; and if you meet a producer then he will certainly be the best producer you will ever meet. Remember that the majority of television people are very temperamental, highly strung and very emotional. I know of one producer who, after a show, enjoys a drink but the tipple seems to bring out a very emotional side of him and sometimes he has been seen crying his eyes out because the show went so *well*!

The point I am making here, and I cannot over emphasize it, is never, *never*, NEVER, criticize the programme you are hoping to appear on. It will definitely be a case of biting the hand that feeds you.

Tony Vick from Leicester was the winner of the 1989 *Countdown* series but he nearly didn't get on the show as he failed the first audition because of a simple slip. He said that he enjoyed the programme but he wasn't terribly complimentary about one of the guest presenters he had seen on a recent edition. Now, his criticism may have been justified, but he broke the golden rule as the people who were holding the audition were quite possibly the ones responsible for employing that guest! Let that be a lesson to you!

But Tony applied again for the show, and this time got through the audition. Being a very clever chap who can do *The Times* crossword in seven minutes, he went through to the final and won. He is now the proud owner of the complete Oxford English Dictionary, all twenty volumes of it.

So be careful at the audition but remember you have nothing to lose and everything to gain. Now, apart from not biting the hand that feeds you, there are some other major things to remember:

1. Enjoy yourself

2. Make sure you have remembered what you wrote on your application form. The interviewers will have that form in front of them when they see you. That is all they have to go on at this stage

3. Remember you have to be your own shop window. Go to the audition as if you are appearing on the show; that is, look smart.

Don't go mad and buy a whole new wardrobe but it will help if it appears that you have made an effort. Also treat yourself to a hair-do . . . that goes for the men as well!

4. Try not to go to the audition straight from work. If you can, get a few hours off work so you can arrive at the audition fresh and bouncy!

5. The best rule is always arrive early . . . never arrive late! Always leave enough time for disasters! If you don't know the area where the audition is being held, then make sure you know how to get there

6. If the host of the show has a famous catch phrase or word, try NOT to do your impression of the host saying the famous words. The interviewers will have heard it all before many times, and it may count against you

7. If the show you are auditioning for requires you and a partner (e.g. *Every Second Counts*) or your family (e.g. *Family Fortunes*) to take part, make sure they all attend. The purpose of the audition is for the production team to meet everyone who may be on their show

8. If the show requires a visual element on your part then try to incorporate it in your audition. For example, if you are applying for *Busman's Holiday* remember that it is a television programme relating to occupations. Recently the production team auditioned three underwater frogmen and they all arrived in their gear, with wetsuits and flippers and all! Another three contestants for *Busman's Holiday* were the manager, deputy manager and beverages manager of the Ritz Hotel who each turned up in top hat and tails together with a rolled copy of *The Times* . . . that's what it's all about!

9. Leave at home all extraneous people
    (screaming children, aunts, uncles, grannies,
    dogs, etc.) who have not applied for the show
    – they will only get in the way and they will
    not be allowed in to the audition room

10. Don't think you are going to meet the star of
    the show because in 99 per cent of the cases
    he or she won't be there. That's what we
    producers are for!

Peter Mason (no relation!) from Upminster in Essex, was
a contestant on *Bob's Full House*. He wrote to the show to
apply to go on, filled in the application form and then had
a two-year wait before he was called for an audition. That
shows how important it is to copy the form. After passing
his audition he then had to wait another six months before
he had a telephone call to say he would be required for
the recording of the show in ten days! Peter's audition
was held at the BBC Television Centre in London. He
told me:

> 'They actually had four of us there all at once,
> just like the game. They first of all chatted to us
> as a group and then took us off one by one into
> a side room and asked thirty general knowledge
> questions just to test our general knowledge. Then
> they brought all four of us back together and asked
> about another twenty general knowledge questions.
> This time we had to shout out the answers to
> see how fast our reactions were and who would
> actually get the answer out first. Then they had a
> very general chat with us and that was it.'

Peter told me his secrets of passing an audition for a
game show.

> 'If you have got a number of rows of chairs at an
> audition, because some auditions are held in large
> numbers, walk straight up to the front and go
> and sit in the front row. Don't sit there grinning

like a Cheshire Cat but go up there and smile and
just basically try to be yourself. Be chatty but not
over-chatty and show them that you're not just
going to sit there and wait to be spoken to. You've
got to offer something up yourself. So sit in the
front row so that people can actually see you. Have
a piece prepared to say about yourself because it is
like being interviewed for a job . . . they will want
to know about you.'

Peter has appeared on *Bob's Full House* and *Strike it Lucky*
but compared to some contestants he is a novice. The Revd
David Smith, Birmingham University Chaplain, is quickly
becoming a professional and admits to having been on six
shows. Like any decent producer would do, as soon as a
vicar complete with dog collar, fun personality and vast
general knowledge walked into the room when we were
auditioning for *Strike it Lucky* we instantly booked him
as a contestant. What we didn't realize until later was the
depth of his experience with regard to game shows. He
had travelled to London to appear on *Fifteen to One* and
Blankety Blank, to Scotland to appear as the first contestant
on *Wheel of Fortune*, to Leeds to appear on *Winner Takes
All*, to Manchester for *Busman's Holiday* and returned to
Scotland for BBC Scotland's *Catchword*. So I thought I had
better to talk to the showbiz vicar about his experiences at
auditions.

'What's the secret of passing an audition?' I asked him.

'Simple,' said the Revd David. 'Number 1, be yourself.
Number 2, enjoy yourself. Number 3, don't be what you're
not. Number 4, have fun.'

'Don't you think your dog collar had anything to do with
your success at auditions?'

'I suppose I do get more attention when I'm wearing it.'

'I suppose you would call yourself a professional game
show contestant now?' I asked.

'Not really,' he replied. 'You see, the game show market
is dying a little at the moment. I think it will pick

Revd David Smith spun the *Wheel of Fortune*. © Scottish TV

up later in the year but at the moment it is a little depressed.'

For a moment I thought I was talking to a stockbroker as he took it all so seriously. 'I'm hopeless at most of the games I have been on,' he continued, 'but when it comes to it I suppose I score zero for playing the game and ten for entertainment value. They call me the King of the Game Shows and there was one newspaper article I saw that said I was the Church of England's answer to Jackie Mason. Now, I have to say I didn't know who Jackie Mason was at the time and I wasn't too impressed, but now I know he is the great American comic I take it as a big compliment.'

'Tell me about the prizes you have won,' I asked.

'Ah, well now, let me see. Basically a bit of money, a *Blankety Blank* chequebook and pen. . . Oh yes, I nearly forgot . . . on *Busman's Holiday* we won an audience with the Pope. Funny that, me being Church of England.'

'Any more tips about passing an audition?' I asked.

'Only to say that most auditions are all the same irrespective of what show you applied for. They're usually held in hotels and in groups. There are a few general knowledge questions and then you have to say a bit about yourself . . . I'm quite good at that bit, you know'.

No wonder he got on!

When you arrive for the audition make sure that the people who are holding it know you have arrived. If you are being auditioned at a hotel tell the reception desk that you have arrived and ask where the auditions are being held. They should know and they should have a list of auditionees and will tick your name off. You should then be directed to a waiting area.

Eventually you will be called in to the audition room and you have a matter of minutes to make your impression. Remember that first impressions are all-important. Many contestant researchers say that they can tell if anyone is going to be any good for their show as soon as he or she walks through the door! But whatever you do, don't go over the top and draw too much attention to yourself.

There was one amusing interlude when *What's My Line?* were holding auditions at a hotel before I joined the show. The contestant researcher went to call in the next auditionee from the gathered hopefuls. She opened the room door, took one look at the people outside and burst into fits of laughter. She had to close the door while she was laughing.

'What's the matter with you?' asked the producer.

'There's a woman out there with a parrot on her shoulder,' she replied, tears now rolling down her cheeks.

'What?' said the producer. 'Let me have a look.'

Sure enough there really was a lady sitting quite non-chalantly with a cockatoo perched on her shoulder! Both producer and researcher were unable to control themselves for a good five minutes before they were able to resume the auditions and call the lady, complete with bird, in to the room for a chat. When she came in, she introduced Corky the Cockatoo. Corky turned out to be quite a marvellous bird that performed on miniature roller skates and then played 'God Save the Queen' with its beak on a miniature piano. Corky and handler were instantly booked for *What's My Line?* and since then Corky has become a star!

The point I am making here is that most of the time first impressions are crucial. Auditions are sometimes very brief and you will only have a short time to make your impression. You see, Corky the Cockatoo could have been brought to the audition in a cage, but he was already on the lady's shoulder and that impact won the day!

To give an example of the numbers of people who apply for shows, in the first week of August 1990 Action Time sent out 10,000 applications for *Wheel of Fortune* but they know that of those 10,000 applicants many won't return the form because they will be put off by its complexity. It is the company's initial filtering system.

Action Time have a very orderly approach to their auditions. The producer of a show will know what he is looking for and will go through the files. They interview at a ratio of up to 10:1 for what they need so if they are looking for fifty contestants they could see at least 500 for that particular show. They interview six people at a time and it takes one hour in a boardroom-type set-up in a hotel and during that time the contestants are given a general knowledge test that is on tape. There are forty general knowledge questions with three seconds' thinking time for each one. The answers are written on a blank sheet of paper and that sorts out the men from the boys. The prospective contestant is also involved in a self-awareness exercise, in which he has to introduce himself to the other contestants. This can be terribly embarrassing for some people, but the fact is that if someone cannot introduce himself in that situation then what will he be like in the studio in front of the presenter, audience and six cameras! The audition then continues with another general knowledge test which is more difficult than anything that will be required on any show.

You may not be surprised to learn that a clinical psychologist devised the Action Time audition, which stresses the contestants then relaxes them. However, from my experience, it is most thorough. Not all auditions are so formal; with *Strike it Lucky* we see three couples every fifteen minutes!

The Krypton Factor requires thirty-six contestants per series plus eight reserves in case anyone drops out for any reason (the most common being contestants hurting themselves on the assault course), so that they need forty-four people from the 10,000 people who apply for the show! The production team use a filtering system, whereby the best 300 are chosen to audition. As the show will be seen all over the country auditionees are chosen from a wide geographical spread as it is only fair that all parts of the country are represented. The contestant researchers then go on 'The Krypton Tour' which lasts for around two weeks. Auditions are held in every major city in the country. Each one lasts for about one hour and eight people are auditioned at one time. The first part consists of a chat and questions on the contestant's health. Then there is a video test. This is almost like playing the game for real, for on the video is the host of the show, Gordon Burns. He puts numerous tests to the hopeful contestants who have to write their answers down. After this video test the audition is over.

It can be seen that at the audition some shows almost play the game that you are hoping to take part in for real. This is exactly the case with *Telly Addicts*. As the show requires families to compete as opposed to individuals, the number of applications is that much fewer. Helen Lott, the contestant researcher of the show, told me that last year they received 2,000 applications from television-mad families. Again, the auditions are held in hotels, and fifteen families are seen during the course of one day. The audition lasts for about twenty minutes during which time a short version of the game is played: clips of various programmes are shown and questions are asked about them ... just like the show itself. The audition continues with a 'spotlight' round where individual members of the families are put through their television knowledge paces.

Other shows that play a brief version of the game at the audition include *Fifteen to One* and *Countdown*. Like *The Krypton Factor*, the personality of the contestants isn't of major importance with these shows. What is important is that the applicants can play the game and play it well. Another factor that producers and contestant researchers will be looking for is how the contestants' nerves bear up under the strain!

Last year 3,500 hopefuls applied to go on *Mastermind*. Peter Massey, the producer, sees about 300 of them individually for twenty minutes each. Unlike the rigid format of the programme, the interviews are informal. General knowledge questions are asked, but it is not necessary to get them all right as all the applicants have to prove, according to Massey, is that their brains are working in the right general area and that they convey their enthusiasm for their specialized subject. He looks out for nervousness at these interviews and his experience can tell him if he may have a problem on his hands.

With speciality shows like *What's My Line?*, auditionees are usually spoken to individually. If it is practical, they usually bring along examples of their work. Normally the contestant will have worked out a mime and this is demonstrated. This audition would last about ten minutes.

Shows that require more of a 'personality contestant' will hold their auditions rather differently. With *Strike it Lucky* two things are important to the producers. One is personality and the other is a good general knowledge. Auditions are normally held in groups of three couples ... as it would be on the show. The audition lasts no more than fifteen minutes and involves a few brief words of introduction followed by a few general knowledge questions. It then moves on to the all-important part, the bit where the contestant has to do the talking. You, the contestant, will be asked all about yourself.

If you are auditioning as a 'personality contestant' be prepared with a short 'routine'. Try to imagine the host of the programme has just asked you to 'tell me all about yourself' on the show for real. Now try to remember all the quirky things that have happened to you, all your odd hobbies and the night the bed collapsed on your honeymoon ... or whatever! The idea is to be remembered, as these types of shows want fun, extrovert people who will be of benefit to the programme. But whatever you do, do not go over the top! For instance, I interviewed a young man for *Strike it Lucky* who had a great sense of humour and a great personality (despite the glitter suit he wore for the audition!) but he just went that little bit too far. As I have said earlier, try to go to the audition as if you were going on the show, but remember that you are not the *star* of the show. This hopeful thought he was going to be. Hence the reason he didn't get on. The star of the show is always the host . . . NEVER try to upstage the star.

On another occasion a lady whom I was auditioning would keep calling me 'young man'. She found it funny, I found it slightly stupid of her to carry on doing this especially after I told her with a degree of firmness that she could call me David. What she did was try to be clever and funny when she wasn't. Remember that the people holding the auditions are like the dragon guarding the cave of treasure. Get past them and the world is your oyster; upset them and you won't stand a chance of getting on the screen!

So, when they ask you to say a few words about yourself make sure you know what you are going to say. They will ask questions about what you have written on your form. Try to guess what they will ask and have an answer prepared. Game shows are fun. It's all a game. Make sure you are fun . . . not dour.

An important note here. There are many interviewing techniques. The interviewers may try to throw you. If there are two, one may be Mr Nice Guy and the other Mr Nasty. Don't take anything they say to heart. Enjoy it all the way. Don't take an obvious dislike to either of them, no matter how difficult it may be. If they say something outlandish about you, simply laugh at yourself. You will be doing that on the show a lot! Many presenters will have fun and a joke with you; the interviewers will simply be seeing how you cope in that situation.

Many companies will pay travelling expenses for attending the audition. For instance, in 1990 *Fifteen to One* paid £15. With *Strike it Lucky* we weren't so generous as we paid each couple £5, but there may be lower-budget shows that just cannot afford to pay anything. My advice is not to expect any recompense for travelling or your time when attending auditions. If some money is offered then accept it gratefully. I would also suggest that you should never ask for more than is offered. This could blot your copybook. As expenses are usually sorted out at the end of the audition, if there is an argument about money then that will be the last thing the production team will remember about you.

At the end of the audition, whatever the show, when you are dismissed do NOT carry on talking to the interviewers while the other contestants are leaving. That will not gain you points. The reason you are leaving is because the interview is over and there are other applicants waiting . . . don't hold things up. Politely say how pleased you were to meet everyone, shake hands and go!

Seven

Preparing

for the

Show

How do you know if you have passed the audition?
Simply, the production office will contact you to tell you
so! From that moment until you appear on the programme
you have some valuable preparation time. This period, if
used wisely, can enhance your chances of doing well on
the show.

From the producer's point of view the time between
auditions and recording the shows is very busy indeed.
I love to have everything written down for the shows I am
involved in producing as I am very forgetful! In our office
we have an enormous board with all the shows we are
recording on it with the dates and times, plus the names
of the contestants we are hoping to put on the show. As
well as their names, we put where they are from, their
relationship and any cryptic note to jog our memories as
to who they were! I always like to keep my options open
up until quite near the date of recording just in case a 'gem'
comes up. So if you have passed the audition for one of the
shows I work on, normally the first letter you receive from
our office is a 'provisional booking' letter.

Basically we tell you that you have been successful in

passing the audition and we are provisionally booking contestants for the series. We give you a date of recording and ask you to ring the office to make sure that that date will be OK with you and your partner. If you have another very important engagement on that particular day then so be it, but remember that there are literally thousands of people who want to get on game shows so try to alter previous arrangements if you possibly can so you can appear on the date given. With our shows if you ring back and confirm that the date is OK then your name changes colour on the board from blue to red. In our office, about three weeks before the show is due to be recorded our secretaries will contact successful contestants to confirm that they are definitely on the show and arrange their travel, hotels and so on for their visit to our studios.

Normally game shows are recorded and, as you will have read earlier in this book, the companies will record up to four or five shows a day depending upon the complexity of the programme. The letter you receive will probably give the programme or show number you are to appear on. Keep that letter. Do not throw it away! Keep it with the copies of your application form and any other correspondence.

It is important to note that if you have been provisionally booked, that is precisely what it means and nearer the date of recording your appearance will be confirmed, but of course there is always the chance that you may be put on 'hold' or 'standby' for the programme. To have standby contestants is quite a normal practice. The idea is that you are on call if someone doesn't turn up. Sometimes you will be paid a nominal fee to be on call by the telephone for a couple of hours a day. When all the contestants have turned up at the studio you will receive a call to say you will not be needed.

As well as normally paying travelling expenses, television companies may pay for a hotel if you live a long way from the studios. If you have to go to the studios by rail then the company may send you the tickets or ask you to get them and they will reimburse you later. Make sure you know how you are going to get there. If you have to buy your own tickets make sure you get receipts so you can present them to the company. Make sure you know how you are expected to travel – first class or second class. Clarify this with your contact at the office, for you don't want any embarrassment and you don't want to be out of pocket! Normally television companies will only pay second-class return fares or a mileage rate if you drive yourself to the studios.

If you decide to drive, ask about parking. Many studios have very restricted parking facilities. Remember that appearing on the show may be a stressful (but enjoyable) experience and after the ordeal you may like to have a drink. That is not compatible with driving. I would suggest that, if at all possible, you let the television company organize your travel, then all you have to do is sit back and enjoy the day!

Obviously you will want to look at your best. When it comes to clothes to wear on television there are a few helpful hints that I can pass on. Firstly, avoid wearing white. It may sound odd, but white clothes will make you look a lot larger on screen than you really are! Goodness knows why this is but it is said that a white suit will put a stone on you. From a technical point of view, white is a very difficult colour to light in the studio as the cameras more often than not cannot cope and you may look 'burnt out', and 'flare' all over the screen. It is an effect that is best avoided!

Herringbone patterns can cause havoc with cameras. Maybe you have seen the effect on your screen. Next time someone is wearing one notice how it constantly changes colour! This is because of something known as an 'interference pattern'. Avoid herringbone patterns.

Colours. Be very careful with colours! If they haven't told you, ask the production office before you go to the recording what colours you can wear. After all, you don't want to be wearing a red dress if the colour of the set is pink!

What does the show involve? Is there a lot of running about? If so, ladies should not turn up in high heels and a tight skirt!

Check all these points with the production office before the recording day. You want the day to be as enjoyable as possible and you want to feel as comfortable as possible. Do not travel in the clothes you want to wear on the show, but travel in something comfortable so you arrive at the studios relaxed. Whatever you do, do not leave your clothes for the show behind at home like one couple did for a recording recently of *Strike it Lucky*. They arrived at 3.00 p.m. for the recording at 7.45 p.m. but during the afternoon they were needed for rehearsal so they couldn't get home to collect their clothes. A taxi was eventually sent to their house with the keys to the front door and finally they got their show clothes about an hour before they were on. They could not possibly have been totally relaxed during the afternoon, which may have affected their chances of winning the game, so it goes to prove that the preparation is all-important if you are to succeed. If necessary, make a list and tick everything off that you should have done, bought or loaded into the car!

Apart from your cosmetic appearance, what else can you do to enhance your chances on the show and make the day that much more enjoyable? David Elias used to be an English lecturer at Nottingham Polytechnic but for the past two years he has been a professional question setter for various quiz and game shows including *The Krypton Factor* and *Quiz Night*. He is well qualified for the job as he is a veteran contestant, having competed in *The Krypton Factor*, *Brain of Britain*, *Sale of the Century* and scores of local radio and TV quizzes. His winnings ranged from a car to a colour TV but possibly the most obscure must have been free pork pies for a year. He says that the secret of his success as a contestant was preparation.

> 'If you are going to appear on a show that involves a buzzer round, it pays to practise and perfect your own buzzer technique. I made up my own buzzer at home . . . it only cost a few pence to make . . . and you'd be surprised how good you can get at it. It sounds daft but the trick is to buzz at the very moment you know what *you think the answer will be.* At that moment you may not have formulated the complete answer in your head but by the time the presenter has said your name and you have to give the answer, then you may have anything up to a three-second advantage over your opponents.'

David tells me that the average reaction time for pressing a buzzer is 0.7 sec. The quicker you can do it the better.

When it comes to answering questions the only way to practise is to get asked some! Possibly the best advice, as I have said earlier, is to join a quiz league. By doing so you will be put into situations where you have to answer questions. Many pubs run quiz leagues and these are fun as well as educational.

Another good tip is to practise *knowing when to guess.* For instance, you may be asked a general knowledge question which no one would be reasonably expected to know. Search around the question; the answer may be hidden in it. David asked me, 'What was the name of a textile dealer from Gloucestershire who became Lord Mayor of London in 1398?' Before I had time to say I didn't know, David continued, 'Not many people would know the date, but this is a classic case of knowing when to guess. There is really only one famous Lord Mayor of London and that was Dick Whittington. That's the answer to the question!'

Whatever your method of preparation, make sure you get yourself mentally prepared. Get a friend to ask you questions. Don't answer them in your head, tell your friend the answer as quickly as you can, as you have to learn to speak out the answers. It sounds odd but this is excellent practice. I remember some twenty years ago I used this 'vocal method' when I was learning Morse code for a radio examination. For three months I would speak out sentences in Morse: Dah–di–dah–dit, dah–dah–di–dah'. People thought I was mad. I may well have been, but I passed. The same goes for you. Not that you're mad, I mean. Always practise, whenever you can. Get quiz books, play Trivial Pursuit, watch shows and call out the answers, brush up whenever and wherever you can.

Bob Louis, chief executive of Atticus Television, was the executive producer of the popular daytime find-the-word game show *Talkabout*, hosted by Andrew O'Connor. Bob told me that after contestants had passed the audition he would set them homework! The show required the contestants to talk about a subject for twenty seconds hoping to hit key words associated with that subject to win points. It is a very skilful game, so Bob sent thirty subjects to all the hopeful contestants, telling them to practise whenever they could, play the game as often as possible . . . at bedtime, in the bath and so on! Although they had passed the first hurdle, auditioning wasn't over yet for when they got to the studio to play the game for real they had to audition again to see how they had got on with their homework . . . except this time it was in front of the show's American consultant! Only if they passed his test did they finally make it next door into the studio to play the game. As Bob told me, 'The game is a very difficult one to play. We didn't want to have any embarrassments. That is why we had to be very careful with our final selection.'

If you have succeeded in getting on to a show where you are a member of a team, before going for the recording make sure you all get together. If you don't know your team-mates very well then now you have some time to do so. If the show requires the team to have a spokesman, work out beforehand which one of you it will be. If you are all meant to have specialized areas as team members then make sure that you all brush up on those areas. You could even try playing the game in a mock-up situation in someone's front room.

For shows that require the contestant to have a degree of physical fitness then make sure you are fit; if you're not, get fit!

Whatever you decide to do to prepare yourself, remember that the day at the studio will be fun and it's all a game anyway!

Eight

The

Television

Studio

Television studios are fun places. As soon as you arrive you will enter a world of entertainment and for one day you will be a star and, hopefully, treated like one! In this new world there is a whole new language and most of the people you meet will be fun, colourful and extrovert. The people that work in the studio all have titles. Whether it be producer or floor assistant, they are all vital to the successful completion of a television production.

If you haven't been to a studio before you may be over-awed with the ritzy-glitzy people with everyone calling each other 'love' (and that's just the fellows!) and it will seem as if there are hundreds of people hanging around not doing anything! Some years ago this may well have been the case but nowadays everyone has an important job to do from the prop man to the producer.

As a contestant it really isn't terribly important for you to know exactly what each and every one in the studio does, but it may help to put you at ease if you know who does what. I mentioned the prop man. Prop men are really called property masters and as the term implies they look after property used in the programme. In the case of a TV studio this means anything that is used by a performer (or contestant) that can be picked up and handled. For example: a toaster, a cuddly toy, a hammer or a balloon.

When one turns the pages of the Thames Television book of apocryphal stories there is a famous tale concerning the day a doctor appeared on a medical programme to discuss the merits of leeches in today's medicine. It was up to the props department to purchase a jar of leeches for him to display on the programme. The leeches were duly purchased and the programme went ahead in Studio Five at Thames's Euston studios, after which props had to dispose of the leeches. They did with them exactly as I would have done, and that was to flush them down the loo. However, an hour or so afterwards a gentleman used the same loo. It has to be said that the gentleman concerned, how can one put it, was more of a man than a wimp, and whilst sitting and contemplating he felt a strange sensation around his delicate areas. Standing up, he was horrified to see three of the leeches, which had obviously refused to be flushed, firmly attached. Having worked on the programme he remembered that they could not simply be pulled off. Deciding that urgent medical attention needed to be sought, he pulled up his trousers and headed for the surgery. As luck would have it, the nurse had gone on another call and had left a secretary to take messages and to tell patients to wait for her to return. The door flew open, the chap with the leeches burst in, dropped his trousers and said to the young secretary, 'Well, what do you think of that, then!'

So that's props. Incidentally, the person who tells props where to put their bits and pieces on the set is normally the stage manager. Stage managers come in all shapes and sizes and can be male or female. As you may have gathered, TV people are sometimes quite eccentric. There was one dear stage manager called Norma who lived up to the eccentricity required. She had a pet kangaroo which she kept in her flat. Quite true. The stage manager usually also organizes outside rehearsals, in other words rehearsals that are not held in the studio but in a rehearsal room.

Now the scene boys, who look after scenery. Scenery is the stuff that is effectively bolted down and doesn't move. Nowadays many dramas are shot on location. If there is a scene of an interior of a house needing to be shot, then the crew will go to a house, but that has not always been the case, for only recently have cameras become small enough to enable crews to use actuality locations. However, there may be situations where it is still more practical to use studios and construct interiors rather than go outside. Soap operas are prime examples but of course wooden walls are not as sturdy as bricks and mortar. For instance *Prisoner of Cell Block H* looks as if it was shot in a Sydney MFI warehouse. Sometimes the illusion of being in a room can be lost when the whole of the set moves! Invariably the walls of Cell Block H rattle and shake when doors are opened and closed.

Scenery is usually very heavy and so if you see some burly chaps around the studio you can bet your bottom dollar (what a good name for a game show!) that they are the scene boys. They have to place it according to the designer's plan for the studio.

The designer is usually very arty and sometimes most temperamental. A designer and his set is rather like a chef with his prize dish. Criticize it and you are heading for trouble. Instead of being hit over the head with a meat cleaver as the chef would do, the designer might burst into tears and throw his pencil at you. Tread carefully. In fact you will probably never meet the designer but we in production work very closely with them as they actually decide what the show's set will look like on screen. It's up to them what the colour and size the set will be and so on.

Probably the most obvious people seen in the studio, apart from the artists and contestants, will be the cameramen. You can spot a cameraman as he wears headphones and is standing behind a camera. It will look at times as if he is talking to himself, indeed most of the time this is the case. Sometimes he may talk to the director of the show who he is listening to through his headphones. The director tells the cameramen where to point the cameras. If things are really going badly then the director may tell the cameramen where they can put their cameras. No, seriously, all the cameramen I have worked with have been great chaps and are very good at their job. However, there is one story I must tell you about one cameraman who was working on *This is Your Life*. The director was well known for playing practical jokes and during the actual recording of the show he shouted over his headphones, 'Quick, Camera 3, give me a close up of Lord Lucan'. Watching his monitors, the director was in hoots of laughter as the camera went to all the faces on the set in turn. Finally in desperation the cameraman spoke to the director and said, 'Which one is he?'

'Oh no,' moaned the director. 'He must have disappeared again . . . don't worry!'

The director is an important chap. He is the one who is responsible for how the programme is shot and thus what it will look like on screen. He may call everyone 'love' or 'darling', and every other word may be a little unsavoury. Sometimes his shirt may be undone to the waist revealing a gold medallion. Directors either smoke heavily or not at all. Either way they are quite easy to spot and will be the one important person who will tell you where to stand and what to do, etc. He will either talk to you himself or will get the floor manager to relay his directions to you.

The floor manager is the man in charge of the studio floor. In TV jargon, when we say 'floor' we don't mean the carpet or the vinyl coverings, we really mean the studio itself. Thus the floor manager may call out, 'Could Michael Barrymore come on the floor now please?' Thus the floor is really the studio or the part of the studio where the production is happening at that moment. Floor managers are quite bossy people and they have to be. TV studios are very expensive places to run and consequently time is money.

The floor assistant is the floor manager's 'runner'. He answers directly to the floor manager and he is responsible for making sure that artists arrive in the studio from their dressing-rooms when they are required for the production. In film studios he is the call boy.

The director usually sits in the box (or gallery) which is another name for the control room, where he has a bank of televisions in front of him showing all the different pictures from the various cameras. He works very closely (sometimes too closely) with his production assistant (usually known as his PA). I remember one PA who complained to me about a director she was working with. She said, 'He's all right but he does treat me like a Fisher-Price activity centre'! The production assistant is the lady who types scripts, times the programme as it is being made, orders-up video tapes, organizes filming, editing, coffee, tea, and does virtually everything. Without the PA we would all be lost. (In the BBC, job designations are slightly different and you may find the PA is a burly chap as the job is somewhat different and is more of an assistant director's role.)

The director tells the vision mixer which shot he wants from which camera and the vision mixer 'punches up' the shot required on the vision mixing panel by pressing the appropriate button. The director is in constant communication with his cameramen, soundmen and the floor manager via 'talkback'. His commands are heard by these people on their talkback radio receivers plugged into which are headphones which they wear. So, if you are a contestant on a show and the director is looking at you on a camera in the box and he would like you to move, to save him coming out of the box on to the floor to tell you he will ask the floor manager to ask you to move. It is a system that works very well and if the floor manager wants to talk to the director then he has a radio transmitter on which he can do just that. That is called reverse talkback. Problems arise if the floor manager is deaf. I used to work with one floor manager who was hard of hearing and the studio was mayhem. Actors were going all over the place and no one had a clue what was going on!

When I first joined Thames TV in 1976 I was blissfully unaware of talkback and the fact that if you spoke in the gallery then your conversation could be sent all over the building via the microphones that are left on in the gallery. I was a very lonely 22-year-old from Suffolk missing Rosemary, my girlfriend (now my wife). After my first day and with stars in my eyes I wanted to telephone Rosemary and whisper sweet nothings. Studio Three (where *Magpie* used to come from) was empty and there was a telephone in the gallery. Ideal, I thought. I dialled the number, Rosemary answered and we had a most intimate conversation. After I put the telephone down the gallery talkback burst into life from all over the building with technicians cracking jokes about our lovey-dovey conversation. They had all been listening and I have never lived it down to this day. Still, who cares?!

I always think of the soundmen as the forgotten few. Everyone usually takes them for granted, and being an ex-sound supervisor myself I sympathize with their plight. However, if you want some good technical advice on, say, a new hi-fi then they are the chaps to chat up! Soundmen operate 'boom' microphones (the ones that are occasionally seen creeping in to the top of a picture on your television) and place individual radio microphones on participants in the show. The sound supervisor is in charge of his crew of soundmen as well as controlling the levels and mixing of sound from the sound control room, usually situated next to the director's box. Also in the sound control room is the grams operator whose job it is to play in to the programme any music or special sound effects from tape machines and discs. Soundmen are generally very sociable and every year at Thames they would organize a terrific Christmas party. At the BBC the same thing is true. One of the BBC's apocryphal stories concerns the time their sound department had a party in one of the studios in Television Centre. There was quite a mess to clear up and the studio was out of action the following day. In their wisdom, the BBC management sent a memo to all the staff saying that under no circumstances will BBC studios be used for entertainment in the future!

Usually situated on the other side of the director's box is the lighting director's box. There is a crew of lighting men associated with every production. The lighting director is in charge of them all and it is he who decides where individual lights will be located in the studio. The lighting crew will place the lights in the correct positions and will also operate 'follow spot lights' during the course of the production. The lighting technicians are called electricians or sparks.

Poles apart from the sparks are make-up and wardrobe. Make-up will plaster rouge all over your face and make you look ten years younger. Bags under the eyes disappear with a wave of a magic brush and even hair can be instantly thickened with a magic spray. A trip into the make-up department can be like a successful trip to Lourdes. Through the doors of make-up can be found the secret of eternal youth, albeit short-lived and in an aerosol can.

Usually next door to make-up, the wardrobe department can be found. Oddly enough there are not that many chaps who work in make-up but in wardrobe it is a different story. In the wardrobe department there are wardrobe mistresses, dressers, and costume designers. These jobs are fairly self-explanatory, the dressers actually dress an artist or actor with the clothes that the costume designer has designed and the wardrobe mistress has sewn together. When you go to a studio as a contestant then you will be asked to bring the clothes you intend to wear. These will normally be taken from you by the wardrobe department who will press anything you require for the show.

The producer is the boss of the whole production. Many people ask the difference between the producer and the director. Simply, the producer is in charge of the finances, the booking of guests for the show and what is ultimately said on the programme, while the director is responsible for transferring the programme from script form to the finished show that we see on screen.

The associate producer usually is the organizer and co-ordinator. Sometimes he is the link between the technical side of making the programme and the artists . . . in this case, you! And, as the job name implies, his main role is to be the producer's main assistant. Sometimes the associate producer is called an assistant producer. Whatever he is called, usually under him he has a team of researchers (who find out information for the programme) and production secretaries.

The researcher is the person who is responsible for gathering information on the artists and – in the case of game shows – the contestants. The researcher may be responsible for the travel arrangements of the contestants and generally looking after their wellbeing on production day.

The production secretary is usually responsible for actually organizing the travel for contestants. This may involve booking a car to take you from A to B as well as sending your rail tickets, etc. The production secretary may well be your main contact in the production office prior to the recording, on the recording day and after recording. Normally she will work very closely with the researcher.

Writers. I nearly forgot the writers. On a game show you can bet that there will be a writer or a team of writers working on the production. They may give you 'feed lines'. These are lines you are asked to say so the host can jump in with a gag. Or you may be asked to recount some funny story which they will note down and pass on to the host who will then ask you about it, by which time the writers may have written some jokes for the host about the story. Writers will usually talk to you during the day before the recording of the show. On the screen credits at the end of a show they may not be credited as writers but as 'Programme Associates' or 'Additional Material by' or 'Programme Consultants'. To give you an example of what a writer may do to make a story amusing, if your name is David Horn, the writers may give the host the gag, 'David, your name reminded me of the time when I took ground rhino horn to increase my sex drive but afterwards every time I saw a Land Rover I chased it.'

Writers have a great ability to work gags into any routine. Like a show I worked on where a young lad said, 'I follow Arsenal Football Club', to which the host replied, 'That's interesting, because I follow girls. You know, last night I followed a girl home. How come she lived at my house and I didn't know about it?' And so it goes on.

Oh, there's the executive producer, too. He's a big boss who usually has more than one production under his control at any one time. Usually he will not be seen as he is the overall administrator of a number of productions. He answers directly to the head of department who in turn answers to the programme controller of the company.

There are lots of other people who work in TV studios but those are the ones that you are most likely to meet. As I have said, knowing a little about what each person does will help to put you at ease on your day in the studio.

Nine
The Show

Show day is the climax of the whole process of applying for a game show. It is when you will make your appearance and sometimes things can go wrong: sometimes things *do* go very wrong! Take for example one Sunday in the late 1960s when *The Golden Shot* was being transmitted live from the ATV studios in Birmingham. The host of the show was Bob Monkhouse and he remembers very clearly (in fact he cannot forget!) that the researchers had made a tiny mistake in selecting a particular contestant. You will remember that the show involved firing crossbows at targets in the studio. Also remember that the show was live and was transmitted on Sunday tea times; having a game show such as this on a Sunday caused a few problems with members of the cloth who occasionally would protest. On one particular transmission one lady contestant was partially sighted, a handicap not compatible with firing crossbows! Bob Monkhouse told me:

'She took aim, fired the crossbow, the bolt went flying up into the ceiling and hit a light. It ricocheted off the light and flew into the audience, hitting a man in the audience who happened to be a lay preacher. He was praying that the show would be taken off the air but he was taken off the air instead! He said that we were showing instruments of the devil on a Sunday afternoon!'

That story, I am assured by Bob, is absolutely true but it did happen over twenty years ago and of course contestant researchers have more experience to draw on now, so there is very little chance of that scenario happening again. Contestant researchers can get clever, though. For instance, Les Dawson remembers well the night he was hosting *Blankety Blank* and the researchers had booked two identical sets of twins without telling him. As soon as he saw one pair of contestants through he turned to welcome the next two and he thought he had flipped for there they were again. As Les said in an interview for *Woman's Own* magazine in 1987, 'Normally the BBC has to make an appointment to see a joke, so this was really unexpected!'

Something else that was unexpected was the night when Des O'Connor had to put his singing skills to good use during a transmission of *Name that Tune* which he was hosting in 1958. The programme, produced by Philip Jones and made at the Granada studios in Manchester was a great success and very popular but one night a contestant caught Des on the hop. The contestant had to identify tunes that were played by the orchestra, and the more tunes identified, the bigger the prize. So with this in mind, Des told the contestant that if he didn't know the tune to say 'pass', then the orchestra would play the next tune and so on. The contestant identified the first two tunes correctly then said 'pass', and kept saying 'pass' until the orchestra had run out of tunes to play. Des, ever the improviser and always professional, immediately started to sing the opening lines to some more songs, the contestant buzzed, guessed the song

Les Dawson cracked the jokes on *Blankety Blank*. © BBC

titles and ended up winning the jackpot ... that's live television for you! Fortunately, most game shows are now recorded so normally the producer would have stopped the show if the orchestra had run out of tunes to play, but that particular edition of *Name that Tune* must have been magical television and compulsive viewing ... well done Des!

Normally you will be very well looked after and all the travel arrangements should go like clockwork. When you arrive at the studios you may be shown to a dressing-room where you can leave your things. Remember that you will be able to change for the recording so don't travel in the clothes you will be wearing on the programme – the producer will want you to look as fresh as a daisy! Remember the hints about clothes and colours in chapter 7. Sometimes the production office will ask you to bring two outfits so that the director will have a choice of what you wear. There may be occasions when the show on which you are to appear has a format which requires the winner to return on the next programme. As you know, some shows record several programmes a day and it may just happen that if you are appearing on one that has a returning champion and you are that person, then the show to which you are to return may be recorded on the same day. You will not want the viewers to think you have just one set of clothes, so normally you would change between the recordings. Whatever the case, the production office should let you know ... and in plenty of time!

During the recording of the 1990–91 series of *Strike it Lucky* we had a bit of fun which proved that many shows are recorded on the same day. We recorded three per evening with Michael Barrymore. It was a very tiring schedule for Michael but he was as fresh on the last show as he was on the first ... just like one of our contestants. Gladys appeared on the programme with her husband, Reginald, and she sang for us when she was interviewed by Michael on the show. Gladys and Reginald appeared in the first show of the evening and all was well. After the recording of their show they both went and sat in the audience to watch the recording of the two other programmes. On the third programme of the evening a young man claimed to be an opera singer but he flatly refused to sing for Michael. Michael called to the audience, 'Anyone up there who can sing for us?'

'Yes, I can,' called Gladys.

Michael yelled out (not knowing who it was who called out), 'Well, come down here and give us a hand.'

Down went Gladys and when Michael saw her he cried, 'Oh, no, not you Gladys, you were on the show six months ago!' That turned out to be a true statement for Gladys's show was transmitted in September 1990 and her return (where she belted out 'Land of Hope and Glory' to the delight of the audience) was shown in February 1991 . . . and naturally, she was wearing the same clothes!

Sometimes the host gives the game away that more than one show is recorded on one day. You may remember on *Play your Cards Right* that the host, Bruce Forsyth, would sometimes say to the audience, 'You're a lot better than last week.' Well, that was simply because they were the same audience as the previous week!

Back to your recording day. Normally there will be a rehearsal before the show is recorded. Sometimes the rehearsals will take place in the afternoon with the recording in the evening in front of a live audience. Make use of the rehearsal. Make sure you understand the rules of the game. Know the geography of the set. If you have any questions ask them in the rehearsals. Don't have any unanswered queries hanging over you. If you are not sure where you are meant to move to, make sure you know before the rehearsal is over. Listen carefully to what you are told.

Peter Mason gave me a most graphic account of his day at the BBC when he appeared on *Bob's Full House*.

'They provided transport from my home in Essex to the studios. A chauffeur-driven car came to my door and picked me up. The other contestants were coming from Scotland and Manchester and were staying at the Kensington Close Hotel. The car took me to the hotel and I arrived at about noon. The production team sorted out the travelling expenses while all us contestants had a drink. After they had done that a fleet of cars then took us on to the BBC Television Centre where we had lunch and another drink. They chatted to us and told us what the arrangements for the day would be and then we sat down and watched a video of *Bob's Full House* just to get the idea of it. Then we had the script writers come in and speak to us and they asked us about our interests and what we liked doing just so they could get the script for when Bob Monkhouse came on to the show. Then we went into afternoon rehearsals. That probably took a couple of hours but we actually rehearsed with Bob Monkhouse. We met him around 3.00 and he chatted to us himself and John Junkin was there as well because he writes for Bob. Then we came out of rehearsals and had something to eat again! We went into wardrobe to get changed and into make-up, and the recording started about 7.30 and finished about 10.00. After the show we went backstage and had a drink and then it was chauffeur-driven car home.

'They recorded two shows that evening. Mine first then another with new contestants. When the show actually starts is the worst bit. You hear the music being played and you think, "My God what am I doing here?" Bob then came on and did his opening spiel and you are sitting there and you get more and more nervous. Once you start, though, you forget about the audience

and the cameras and you play the game. I
thoroughly enjoyed it and Bob put me completely
at ease.'

Bob Monkhouse firmly believes in putting contestants at
ease and says that he makes a conscious effort to become
the contestants' best friend and he remembers what Paul
Daniels once told him. Paul always tells his contestants
on his shows, 'This is not real life. It is all fun and it's
all fiction. Look terrific, be a good sport but remember
it's all pretend.' Bob borrowed that little speech and uses
it when he talks to his contestants. When Bob saw Paul
recently he told him that he always uses his speech to
which Paul replied, 'Oh, I stopped saying that myself
years ago.'

However, Paul still puts his contestants completely at
ease on *Every Second Counts* for he is with them most
of the day of recording. After Paul and the contestants have lunched together he shows them a video of
the show followed by what can only be described as
a complete TV lecture. In forty-five minutes he tells
them about camera angles, sound equipment, who does
what, why certain things are done in a TV studio and
so on. 'But,' he told me, 'I always tell contestants that
the number one rule is, "If anything happens that you
don't understand and may affect your chances in the
game, then stop the show – even on the recording. After
all the technical crew stop the show often enough, so
if you're not happy say so."' His speech which he passed on to Bob has been modified a little. He now tells
his contestants, 'Today is not real. Whatever happens
today it is not going to change the world. If you lose,
don't worry. Remember the British public love a loser.'

Max Bygraves told me that he always put his contestants
at ease in rehearsals when he was hosting *Family Fortunes*
by asking silly questions. One of them was, 'Where would

you find mangoes?' and his answer to that was, 'Where a woman goes!' His favourite story about rehearsals concerns an Irish family who were all girls – a mother and her four daughters. Max asked them: 'Captain Cook sailed around the world three times. Which voyage did he die on?' to which the mother replied, 'Don't ask me, I'm no good at geography.'

Max Bygraves offered 'Big Money' on *Family Fortunes*.
© Central TV

Max remembers the show with great affection. His catch-phrase on the programme was 'Big money' (which has to be said with a shake of the lower arms!); it was Max himself who thought it up. They recorded two shows a night and did four or six shows a week. Nowadays that is not a heavy workload. As I am sure you know, *Family Fortunes* is a game based on the answers given to silly questions by 100 people. The contestants consist of two families of five people. Nerves can be a problem as a contestant from Hoddesdon in Essex discovered. Max asked him, 'Name something you'd take on the beach with you' to which he replied 'A turkey'. Max asked him his next question, 'Name an animal that climbs trees'. He said 'turkey' again. It didn't matter what question he asked this man, all he could reply was 'turkey'. So Max asked him why did he keep doing that. The man explained that he knew the answer to the first question was towel; he wanted to say 'Turkish towel' but it came out as turkey, and he got stuck on the word because of his nerves.

After the show his wife went up to Max and said to him, 'Wasn't he disgraceful? How much would you take not to put it on?' Max consulted Bill Stewart the producer and Bill jokingly asked her what sum did she have in mind. The wife replied, '£100.' Bill then had to explain that one edition of the show cost £38,000 to mount. 'Well, he most definitely isn't worth that,' she said. 'Put it out!'

Through the series of *Family Fortunes* there have been some hilarious categories. Possibly the best *double entendre* must have been 'we asked 100 people what would a man have in his hand when he is walking down the street'. (The top answer was a letter!)

Family Fortunes still remains a top-rating show. It started life in this country with Bob Monkhouse as host, then came Max, but since 1987 it has been Les Dennis who has asked the questions. Les has a collection of stories about the show. He told me about the time there was a celebrity edition being recorded. Barry McGuigan was asked 'Name something money couldn't buy', to which Barry replied, 'Our tractor.' Then Les told me about the family who all worked at GCHQ, (the government communications headquarters). When Les interviewed them before the start of the game every question he asked them

Les Dennis, current host of *Family Fortunes.* © Central TV

about themselves they said they couldn't answer because of the Official Secrets Act! However, his favourite story is the one about the lady who was going for the jackpot. If the answer she gave wasn't on the board then Les told her he would say 'Again' and she should think of something else to say. 'Name something red,' said Les to which she replied, 'A tomato'. 'Again,' said Les. 'TOMATO!' she shouted out!

One popular game show that started life here in the UK in the summer of 1988 was *Wheel of Fortune*. The show is based on a very successful American format and is made here by Scottish Television for the ITV Network, hosted by Radio One DJ Nicky Campbell. Normally two or three shows are recorded a day at the studios in Glasgow. As with 99 per cent of all networked shows the contestants come from all over the country. Nicky Campbell likes to meet them before the show and take them through the rehearsals. Normally there are rehearsals in the morning at the studios and everyone gets a chance to play the game and pick up hints and tips. The biggest tip Nicky passes on is how to actually spin the wheel. It looks easy but it takes a lot of practice to get it just right.

Nicky told me that although the contestants have gone through the rigorous mechanism of selection some are terribly good in rehearsals and then they freeze for the show, but more often than not the reverse is true. It is during the rehearsals that Nicky chats to the contestants to find out bits and pieces about them. One day one of the contestants was a 6ft 3in bouncer and while he was having some make-up put on Nicky heard him say that his mates would give him a hell of a time if they saw him with all 'that stuff' on his face. When he came on for the recording Nicky established in the interview that he was a bouncer and then said, 'By the way, your mascara's running!' Fortunately for Nicky, he won the game.

Spin the wheel and win a prize with hostess
Carol Smillie and host Nicky Campbell. © Scottish TV

Having presented forty or so editions, Nicky is experienced enough to offer new contestants some advice. He
told me what he expects of a good contestant:

'You've got to be lively, have a real sense of fun
and enter into the spirit of the game. It is no use
going on the show and standing there behind the
wheel or podium and saying to yourself, "I'm just
here to win and the only reason I'm on this show
is because I want to win the car." That goes against
the purpose of the whole thing. Winning should

be a bonus, the icing on the cake. The real fun, the real experience is that long after you have spent the money or the car's knackered you'll remember the day in the TV studio and the day of the game show. I personally love it. Every day I spend in the studio I love it. You do sometimes get people who are in it for the wrong reasons.'

Television personality and quiz show host Angela Rippon agrees to some extent with Nicky Campbell's views. She says:

'Winning is very important to some people; they don't like to be beaten. A lot of people would come on the show and enjoy it for the pleasure that it gives them to be on it, but an awful lot of them are determined to win. The programme that I presented called *Masterteam*, which was a team version of *Mastermind*, had a team of three appearing on it who were determined to wipe the floor with everybody else and they didn't. They got beaten and one member of the team was so miffed at having been beaten he actually cheated, not in the way he answered the questions but by tipping off the other teams playing that day. One of the beaten team members walked back into the green room where the other teams were waiting ready to go and said in a very loud voice, "Gosh that bloke on the end (and said his name) was absolutely brilliant at pop music" and then clapped his hand over his mouth in mock horror and said, "Oh I shouldn't have said that". But he had revealed the identity of the pop music specialist and so the teams playing against the pop genius never gave him a chance to answer any questions on his specialist subject.

'You see,' said Angela, 'for some people it is only a game until you lose.'

Angela has presented many quiz and game shows and I recently worked with her on a series of *What's My Line?*

Last year a woman appeared on the show who trained a team of boxer dogs to play football. We finished the programme with the dogs playing with a balloon as the ball. Dog-football rules dictate that a goal is scored when the balloon bursts, after which another balloon is thrown in and the game starts again. The idea was that Angela would sit on the corner of the set and do a running commentary on the match, but as she sat on the floor the boxers decided that she was fair game and wanted to play, so the whole football team leapt on her and licked her all over. As Angela said, 'Boxers are very heavy dogs!' Instead of the game of football it was a romp with Angela that the viewers saw.

For some shows you will not meet the presenter until the recording proper, not because he or she doesn't like you but because it adds spontaneity to the show. The presenter will then be able to 'bounce' off you and have a good interview with you. To rehearse an ad lib interview is the worst thing that can happen. This is a common occurrence in America but Bob Monkhouse told me a horror story about one American host who refuses to read anything about or meet his contestants before the show. Bob met this man and asked him, 'What happens if they are talking too much or they get a bit cocky and you need to stop them?'

'Oh,' said the presenter, 'I use the mouth tear.'

'What is a mouth tear?' asked Bob.

The presenter then described how he puts his thumb in the contestant's mouth and grabs the side of their cheek. Because of the camera angles it looks as if he has a friendly hand on the contestant's shoulder, not grabbing hold of his mouth! The presenter went on to explain that he has never been bitten yet and all his contestants are well behaved! I just can't imagine Magnus Magnusson doing that, somehow!

Mouth tear or not, remember to ENJOY your day. You will be looked after and hopefully when you play the game, whatever it is, you will win lots of prizes.

After the show is aired you will go through a period when you may be recognized in the street, especially if you live in a small community. Normally the local press will feature local people who appear on television and you may find your photograph plastered all over the *Esher News and Mail* or the *Knotty Ash Gazette*. After all, you will be big news . . . for a few days.

Being a star can have its pitfalls, though. A contestant was arrested after appearing on *What's My Line?* in 1951. He had given his occupation as a frogman but a bank manager watching the show called the police when he recognized the man as someone who had passed a dud cheque at his bank! The moral is, don't rob a bank until after you have appeared on TV!

Enjoy your days of stardom. It doesn't happen to everyone. But remember that possibly the reason you are there is because you knew a few things about the way game shows are produced and a few inside secrets from this book.

PS. Now you've done it once, apply again for another show. There are many people who do and are successful at it. The more auditions you attend the better you get at it, and the more shows you will be invited to appear on.

Ten

The Future
of the
Game Show

It is very difficult to predict exactly what the future of the game show will be. Obviously with more television channels there will be more demand for all types of programmes which will presumably include game shows, especially considering the economics involved in producing them. David Elstein, director of programmes for Thames Television, told me that they will continue to be an economic proposition as some good peak-time shows attract 12–14 million viewers at a cost per show of £15,000 to £75,000.

The cheaper you make the show, and as long as the popularity remains, then you make more money from it. But as Elstein says, 'You cannot clutter up the schedules with too many game shows'. The reason for this is that viewers will get bored with them. However, Elstein is always looking for new formats although his favourite is the old American show *Tell the Truth*. He believes that there is an element of truth in the theory that the times are changing, and instead of Europe looking towards America for game show formats, America is now looking towards Europe. Most formats that have been bought from the USA have been on air for some time so the show would have been a tried and tested product. This is where the problem lies insomuch as it is far easier for a programme controller to commission a show that is tried and tested rather than going for something new as he would have to develop the format and hope the audience likes it at the end of the day. America had, for years, a wealth of tried shows on air on literally hundreds of TV channels. This mountain of material has all but dried up and now the tables are being turned. For example, Chris Tarrant's high-tech computer game show, *Everybody's Equal* has been sold to the USA.

John Bishop, assistant head of variety at the BBC, doesn't think that the changes in the European market in 1992 will mean that the game show will have to have more of a European flavour, but programme makers will have to address themselves to providing material for that future market. As John pointed out to me, the problem with European game shows is that they tend to be a mixture of a variety show and a game show. If a game show has to put in variety acts in order to make the programme entertaining then there has to be something basically wrong with the game itself. John told me that good home-grown game shows are hard to find. One of the most successful that the BBC have found and produced has been the bingo general knowledge game *Bob's Full House*, and this has been sold to a major producer in the USA, Lorimar Productions. This is a sign of things to come.

Europe is becoming a creative centre but not many pan-European game shows are likely to materialize, for there are barriers of language and culture, and with those two significant problems come those of taste and humour. John Fisher, head of variety at Thames Television, likens this situation to that of local newspapers: what is of interest and fun to a local newspaper in one area will not be of interest to a local newspaper in another.

Henry Kelly puts the question to 'Go for Gold'. © BBC

However, pan-European quiz *shows* exist now, for example *Going for Gold*, but of course the game relies on the fact that the European contestants can speak English. So as far as quizzes go, and so long as the contestants speak a common language, then we can have a pan-European show. But with game shows things are a little different. What makes a Spaniard laugh doesn't make a Belgian laugh. (Come to that I doubt if anything would make a Belgian laugh!) But of course the biggest problem is that of language. To even suggest that there should be one European television language could possibly start the reconstruction of the Berlin Wall! Of course we all remember the European game show without words but with huge dolls and twenty-foot footballs, *Jeux Sans Frontières*, so another along these lines will probably be the extent of things to come in Europe; obvious, bland humour will break down any barriers, hence the reason why the Benny Hill shows sell worldwide!

With high-tech world-wide communications could come high-tech global games. It won't be too long before we see 'the big one' on our screens. As more people are equipped with touch-tone telephones in their homes then we could see the ultimate television game show. That is the one where every viewer can play and have the possibility of winning through keying in his answers to questions via the telephone while watching the show on television. *Everybody's Equal* was the show that went some of the way to the ultimate game show inasmuch as the whole studio audience were able to play the game by pressing their answers on individual audience touch pads. John Fisher believes the first step to this ultimate goal may be via a card system whereby a viewer could buy a copy of, say, the *TV Times*, inside which is a coded card which when placed into a device in the home allows interactive play with a game on TV.

Action Time is synonymous with game shows in Europe, and the company's boss, Stephen Leahy, regularly flies

Action Time boss Stephen Leahy. © *Times* Newspapers

to Russia to negotiate with Soviet television on co-production deals on game shows. This is obviously a new market only recently opened to Western television producers. Stephen's travelling has paid off for Soviet television screened its first-ever game show at 9.45 p.m. on 12 January 1991 and it was an Action Time show called *Love at First Sight*. The match-making show was an instant hit with the 180 million Russian viewers, for they had never seen anything like it before! The show was unique for a number of reasons. It was shot in England at the Nottingham studios of Central Television but taped completely in Russian. The audience consisted of Russian-speaking people from Leeds and Nottingham Universities. The whole production team flew in from Russia as did the presenter and the three boys and three girls who competed. In order that the crew knew what was happening they were all equipped with radio ear pieces through which a simultaneous translation was heard. Stephen actually devised *Love at First Sight* himself and the English version can be seen on British Sky Broadcasting where it is No. 1 in the ratings.

But does Britain look towards Europe for game shows? Stephen Leahy believes that Britain doesn't think that Europe has anything to offer, but he knows they have. He buys shows from all over the place! When I interviewed him in the summer of 1990 for this book I asked him if, when Britain enters Europe in 1992, that will make a difference to game shows, to which he replied that if anything is going to happen then it is happening now. 'People who are going to do it in 1992 are doing it now,' he said. Although many European countries have formats on offer that we can adapt, they generally do not know what they are producing themselves and they require a great deal of help from experienced game show producers. To this end Leahy can be found flying all over Europe consulting on different shows.

East met West when Action Time produced this
Russian version of *Love at First Sight*. © Action Time

One thing is for sure in the future, and that is that the
prize levels on game shows in this country will increase
dramatically. While writing this book it was announced
that from 1993 cash limits on game show prizes are to
be scrapped on commercial radio and television stations.
Game shows are also to be allowed to feature prizes
marketed by programme sponsors of the shows.

The world's your oyster. Go for it!

Appendix 1

Principal game shows and their makers

For contact telephone numbers and addresses simply look up the name of the maker in Appendix 2.

Please note that this list was compiled in 1991. Television production schedules do change so it will be worthwhile to telephone the appropriate company to make sure that the show you want to apply for is still in production before writing away for an application form. New shows are always in the pipeline so keep a lookout for press advertisements and on-screen advertising for contestants.

Busman's Holiday   Action Time
Presenter: Sarah Kennedy

Contestants: Three teams of three workmates all in same occupation, e.g. florists, undertakers, waiters, etc., competing against each other.
Game Outline: Questions are asked about own occupations and the occupations of the other two teams competing. Other questions on geography . . . two

countries chosen from a possible six that the teams have
been briefed on.
Prizes: Winning team wins a European holiday but if that
team wins the final round which involves one member
of the team answering questions on just one country
then the whole team wins a world trip.

Connections   Action Time
Presenter: Simon Potter

Contestants: Outgoing personalities who are good lateral
thinkers. Age group 18 to 55.
Game Outline: A sophisticated quiz based on lateral
thinking where three contestants are asked to find the
connection between a series of visual images.
Prizes: Cash, with a limit of £400.

Love at First Sight   Action Time
Presenters: Bruno Brooks and Helen Brumby

Contestants: Lively, outgoing personalities must be
single. Mostly 18–30 age group but an occasional
over–50 show.
Game Outline: Billed as the most candid TV
relationship game show, three men and three women
choose their ideal partner for a night out. Compatible
couples have a date and are invited back to the studio
the next day to reveal all.
Prizes: Love trips to exotic destinations.

Remote Control   Action Time
Presenters: Anthony H. Wilson and Frank Sidebottom

Contestants: Extroverts with knowledge of cultural trivia,
aged 18 to 24 years.
Game Outline: An anarchic combination of comedy and
quiz with three contestants put through five gruelling
rounds. They are questioned on popular culture and
the eventual winner goes through to a solo round in the
infamous spinning wheel where they have to identify
nine celebrities from photographs.
Prizes: Joke prizes, mostly from junk shops!

Runway   Action Time
Presenter: Richard Madeley

Contestants: Three per show. Bright and worldly
with good personalities, travelled, variety of ages,
backgrounds, etc.
Game Outline: General knowledge with strong travel
element.
Prizes: Travel related, up to a travel voucher to the value
of £600.

Lucky Ladders   Anglia Television
Presenter: Lennie Bennett

Contestants: 2 related couples per show.
Game Outline: Word game. 7–rung word ladder, word
at top, word at bottom of ladder. Clues are given to fill
in the missing related words, e.g. Top word ® Cheese,
Bottom word ® Typist, then the ladder would go:
Cheese, Chalk, French, Language, Foreign, Office, Typist.
The two related couples compete against each other.
Prizes: Holidays.

Jumble   Anglia Television
Presenter: Jeff Stevenson

Contestants: 2 per show who team up with celebrity
partners to play against each other.
Game Outline: A cartoon and a cryptic clue are given
which has to be unjumbled to reveal a mystery phrase.
Contestants have to be good at unravelling mystery
phrases and words.
Prizes: Holidays.

Everybody's Equal   Celador Productions
Presenter: Chris Tarrant

Contestants: Whole studio audience of 200 take part.
Game Outline: Computer assisted game where each
audience member has a control pad onto which answers

to questions are tapped in. Elimination game. As game progresses so the number of audience taking part is diminished to just 10, after which the final round reveals the winner.
Prizes: £2,000 max cash prize to the winner.

Blockbusters   Central Television
Presenter: Bob Holness

Contestants: Clever, bright, 16–18 year olds selected after their head teachers or college principals have written to *Blockbusters* and the students pass the audition.
Game Outline: Fastest-on-the-buzzer general knowledge educational quiz show where the contestants, 2 against 1, make their way around a scoreboard which lights up as they give the correct answers to questions on a variety of topics. Aimed at a school-age audience, but *Blockbusters* is very popular with adults.
Prizes: Each contestant receives an electronic personal organizer, dictionary and special *Blockbusters* sports shirt. All prizes related to educational and improvement subjects including educational trips around the world.

Bob's Your Uncle   Central Television
Presenter: Bob Monkhouse

Contestants: Newly married couples.
Game Outline: Game played by the couples in full wedding dress! A Saturday night show which is a fun, active run-around show with trivia questions.
Prizes: Top prize of a car plus various 'wedding presents'.

Bullseye   Central Television
Presenter: Jim Bowen

Contestants: Outgoing relaxed individuals with good all-round general knowledge. Must be good darts players and show steady nerve under pressure.

Game Outline: Jim Bowen asks the questions of three
pairs of contestants per show and they display their
skills around a dart board. A guest darts player appears
on every show and wins money for charity.
Prizes: Cars, speedboats and cash up to about £500.

Family Fortunes   Central Television
Presenter: Les Dennis

Contestants: Cheerful personalities, bright and lively,
above all quick-witted contestants – all related. Very
strong family theme so they have to get on with each
other! Ten contestants per show – two families of five.
Game Outline: Two families against each other in a
fact-fun format.
Prizes: 'Big money' prizes of £3,000 plus spot prizes.

The $64,000 Question   Central Television
Presenter: Bob Monkhouse

Contestants: Individuals with strong specialized
knowledge on one subject – 'From Star Trek to Spurs'.
Game Outline: *Mastermind* with money.
Prizes: Doubling prize money system as the questions
get harder. Maximum £6,400.

Pyramid Game   Chapter One Productions
                          (daytime ITV)
Presenter: Steve Jones

Contestants: 2 teams comprising member of public with
celebrity partner.
Game Outline: The teams compete against each other in
this fast and furious word game. A maximum of 7 words
come up on a screen which the team partner has to
guess by his partner saying words associated with it but
without saying the actual word. Each contestant has six
goes at each word that appears. First rounds win points.
The team with the maximum points go through to the

jackpot pyramid game where phrases are described to
the partner who has to guess what the phrase is, thus
building up the answers on a pyramid.
Prizes: Maximum of £3,000 per week.

The Crystal Maze   Chatsworth Television
Presenter: Richard O'Brien

Contestants: 6 individuals per show. Have to be
physically agile, strong personalities, good general
knowledge, generally bright. Age range 16 to 40.
Game Outline: Adventure game show that takes
the contestants through the crystal maze. A mental
challenge show where the contestants have to solve a
series of challenges, each one in 2 to 3 minutes. The
more challenges solved buys more time in the crystal
dome where tokens are won. The more gold tokens
collected, the bigger the prize. Silver tokens have to
be avoided as these are deducted from the total of gold
ones collected.
Prizes: Adventure trips or holidays. The more gold
tokens the better the trip or holiday.

The Krypton Factor   Granada Television
Presenter: Gordon Burns

Contestants: 4 individuals per show. Age and sex
immaterial just as long as they are physically fit.
Physical strength, good mental agility and good general
knowledge essential.
Game Outline: The game involves a test of physical
fitness on an assault course, mental agility tests,
observation tests, manual dexterity tests, general
knowledge round.
Prizes: Trophy to overall winner of the series.

Quiz Night   Granada Television
Presenter: Martin Roberts

Contestants: Teams taken from pub quiz leagues from all
over the country.

Game Outline: General knowledge team quiz game.
Prizes: Non-reward show.

Blind Date   LWT
Presenter: Cilla Black

Contestants: Single ladies or men in search of a partner.
Age range 18 to 80.
Game Outline: 3 men (or ladies) compete for a date with
a lady (or man) by replying to questions put by the lady
or man in search of an ideal partner.
Prizes: A date with the chosen partner which is filmed
and shown on the following week's programme. The
date could be anywhere from a Caribbean beach holiday
to a day at the zoo.

Fifteen to One   Regent Productions
Presenter: William G. Stewart

Contestants: Fifteen individuals compete against each
other in this knock-out general knowledge quiz. Good
general knowledge is all that is required.
Game Outline: On answering a question correctly a
contestant can elect another contestant to answer the
next question. Each contestant has three lives. Three
wrong answers and that contestant is out of the game
until just three are left in the final round where the
winner is discovered. Winners go on the winner's board
where a running total shows the highest winner for
the series.
Prizes: A trophy or statue for the series winner.

Going for Gold   Reg Grundy Productions
Presenter: Henry Kelly

Contestants: 7 individual contestants per show
chosen from 18 countries. There is always a UK

contestant. Main requirement is good general knowledge.
Game Outline: General knowledge knock-out game.
Prizes: A far-away holiday.

Jeopardy   Reg Grundy Productions
Presenter: To be announced

Contestants: 3 individual contestants per show. Good general knowledge is the main requirement.
Game Outline: Answers are given to which the contestant has to give the questions.
Prizes: Various cash prizes.

Key Notes   Reg Grundy Productions
Presenter: Alistair Duval

Contestants: 2 teams of three. Teams put together at studio. Individuals apply. Good music knowledge.
Game Outline: Music quiz. Contestants have to identify a piece of music after hearing only a few notes.
Prizes: Various cash prizes.

Sale of the Century   Reg Grundy Productions
Presenter: Peter Marshall

Contestants: 3 individuals per show competing against each other.
Game Outline: Money won for successfully answering general knowledge questions. During show, sale-priced goods are offered to the contestants which they can buy with their winnings. At the end of the game the contestant with the most money goes through to final.

Prizes: Various household goods. Maximum prize
is a car.

Wheel of Fortune   Scottish Television
Presenter: Nicky Campbell

Contestants: 3 individual adult contestants per show.
Game Outline: Based on the parlour game Hangman
but modified for screen. 'Either/or' general knowledge
questions are put to the contestants which, if answered
correctly, gives the contestant a spin of the wheel which
reveals a point prize or you can go bust, depending
upon where it lands. Letters are then put into a grid
to reveal a well-known phrase or saying. If guessed the
game is won, or tactically the game continues in order
for the contestant to gain more points.
Prizes: Household goods, a car, luxury holidays.

Win Lose or Draw   Scottish Television
Presenter: Danny Baker

Contestants: 2 teams comprising 2 male celebrities
and one male contestant competing against 2 female
celebrities and one female contestant.
Game Outline: *Give us a Clue* with pictures instead
of mimes. Team member draws a picture, fellow team
members have to guess what the saying that goes with
the picture is. Based on the game Pictionary.
Prizes: On average cash prize of £200 to winner.

Funhouse   Scottish Television
Presenter: Pat Sharp

Contestants: 2 teams comprising a boy and a girl from
different schools.
Game Outline: Adventure game combined with general
knowledge. The team that wins the highest amount of
points gets into the funhouse.
Prizes: Transistor radios, etc., and adventure holidays.

Strike it Lucky   Thames Television
Presenter: Michael Barrymore

Contestants: Bright personalities. 3 couples. Each
couple either related or workmates, etc. Contestants very
important in this highly successful format. Good general
knowledge required.
Game Outline: Based on general knowledge, correctly
answered questions lead the contestants across a bank
of television monitors revealing prizes and menacing
'hot spots'.
Prizes: Cash prizes up to £3,000 jackpot plus other
smaller prizes *en route*.

Take Your Pick   Thames Television
Presenter: Des O'Connor

Contestants: Chosen from the studio audience but have
to be lively, outgoing individuals.
Game Outline: The degree of success the contestants
achieve in the famous 'Yes/No' interlude determines
the order in which they appear for the second part of
the show where, after answering three simple general
knowledge questions correctly, the contestant can either
open a box revealing a prize or take the money that the
presenter offers for the key that opens the box, forfeiting
the unknown prize.
Prizes: Variety of household goods and holidays, but
also there are a few booby prizes!

What's My Line?   Thames Television
Presenter: Angela Rippon

Contestants: Age, looks and personality immaterial.
Interesting and odd occupations are the only
requirement.
Game Outline: A panel of celebrities have to guess the
occupation of the contestant from a simple, short mime
and the contestant answering up to 10 questions from
the panel which he can only answer 'yes' or 'no'.

Prizes: If the contestant beats the panel he wins a
certificate.

All Clued Up   Television South (TVS)
Presenter: David Hamilton

Contestants: 2 married couples per show. Have to be
good at solving word puzzles.
Game Outline: Played by solving well-known phrases
or sayings using a variety of word clues and utilizing a
giant typewriter keyboard to key in letters into a grid.
Prizes: Top prize of £500 and other smaller prizes.

Catchphrase   Television South (TVS)
Presenter: Roy Walker

Contestants: 2 lively individuals per show. Usually male
and female.
Game Outline: Computer graphics are generated
which form a well-known phrase. The quickest on the
buzzer to identify the phrase wins cash amounts. The
contestant with the most winnings after the first game
goes through to the final game where 25 letter squares
are displayed. Behind each letter is a graphic which the
competitor has to identify as a phrase. If the contestant
gets a line of these going through the centre 'M' square
then he or she wins the jackpot.
Prizes: Cash prizes plus jackpot, typically 'far away'
holidays.

Concentration   Television South (TVS)
Prizes: Nick Jackson

Contestants: From a wide range of backgrounds and age
range from 18 to 80. Outgoing personalities and good
memories. Two contestants per game.
Game Outline: A game board featuring numbered
squares has a prize behind each number and contestants
try to match up the prizes. A picture puzzle is gradually
revealed.

Prizes: Holiday for two is star prize, together with smaller prizes.

Tell the Truth   Television South (TVS)
Presenter: Fred Dinenage

Contestants: 6 individual people in two rounds.
Game Outline: 3 contestants stand up in turn in front of a celebrity panel and declare that they are a certain person (e.g. 'I am an opera singer'). Only one of the three is right and the panel have to guess which one. For the third round the four 'bluffers' from rounds one and two go to round three where they all declare they have done the same unusual thing (e.g. 'I have climbed Mount Everest'). Only one is telling the truth and the panel have to guess which one it is.
Prizes: No prizes. *Tell the Truth* is a non-reward show.

Crosswits   Tyne Tees Television
Presenter: Tom O'Connor

Contestants: 2 individual contestants with celebrity partner. One male and one female contestant per show. Have to be crossword buffs.
Game Outline: Crossword puzzle game. The aim is to solve clues on the crossword that lead to solving a key word that connects all six clues in a round.
Prizes: Holiday breaks to the value of £500.

Chain Letters   Tyne Tees Television
Presenter: Alan Stewart

Contestants: 2 lively, outgoing personalities per show compete against each other.
Game Outline: The Chain Letters computer, 'Wordsworth', generates a four letter word. The contestants have to change the word, one letter at a time, to make another word.
Prizes: Cash prizes up to £1,000.

Countdown   Yorkshire Television (Channel 4)
Presenter: Richard Whiteley

Contestants: 2 contestants compete against each other
in this word and maths game. Contestants have to be
instant lexicographers and mathematicians. Age and sex
immaterial.
Game Outline: Letters are picked at random from which
the contestant who can make the longest word wins the
round. Also there is the number round where numbers
are picked at random and a computer generates a
figure. The numbers picked are than added, subtracted,
multiplied and divided by the contestants to reach the
number picked by the computer. The contestant who
does so wins the round.
Prizes: Overall series winner wins a set of dictionaries.

Wife of the Week   Yorkshire Television
Presenter: Christopher Biggins

Contestants: 4 wives with their husbands.
Game Outline: Silly fun games for married couples.
Through the games it is discovered how much the wife
knows about the husband. The wife who knows her
husband best out of those couples competing is declared
the winner.
Prizes: TBA at time of going to press.

Talkabout   Yorkshire Television
Presenter: Andrew O'Connor

Contestants: 2 couples per show. Tough auditions that
guarantee only quick thinkers and wordsmiths compete.
Game Outline: A topic is given for the contestant to talk
about. In 30 seconds the competitor has to say as many
words about the topic as possible. There are 10 key
words that he or she has to say to win the round. If he
fails to hit the key words then the topic is passed on to
the competing couple to try to find all the missing key
words.

Prizes: Various cash prizes with the possibility of an open-ended prize accumulator through series.

Big Break   BBC Television
Presenter: Jim Davidson

Contestants: 3 individuals per show. Must be over 18. Each contestant teams up with a star snooker player to play the game.
Game Outline: By answering general knowledge questions, the contestants win time. In the time won his or her snooker playing partner has to pot as many balls as possible. Each ball potted wins a prize.
Prizes: Various cash prizes plus top prize of a holiday.

Every Second Counts   BBC Television
Presenter: Paul Daniels

Contestants: 3 husband and wife couples.
Game Outline: General knowledge questions are asked and for each one answered correctly time is won. The couple with the most amount of time won at the end of the game go through to the jackpot round.
Prizes: Mystery star prize – usually a holiday.

The Generation Game   BBC Television
Presenter: Bruce Forsyth

Contestants: Related couples of opposite sex. Generation gap must be at least 16 years. Husband and wife teams not accepted.
Game Outline: Fun activity game where the contestants have to take on the professionals at their own game.
Prizes: Consolation prizes plus jackpot conveyor belt where the goods won can be anything from a cuddly toy to a holiday.

Takeover Bid   BBC Television
Presenter: Bruce Forsyth

Contestants: 3 individuals per show.

Game Outline: Each contestant is given a selection of
prizes before the show begins. These prizes are used
to bid against each other after answering crazy cryptic
questions. Winner of cryptic round goes through to final
general knowledge round.
Prizes: Household goods and a top prize which is
usually a holiday.

Fast Friends   BBC Television
Presenter: Les Dawson

Contestants: Two team captains pick up to 3 'friends'
from the studio audience to help answer general
knowledge questions.
Game Outline: Two teams play for the major
prize of a holiday by answering a series of questions in
an elimination contest, winning prizes along the way.
Prizes: Top prize of a holiday.

Telly Addicts   BBC Television
Presenter: Noel Edmonds

Contestants: Four members of the same family.
Game Outline: Two teams consisting of two families
compete in this television quiz about television. Various
rounds identifying artists, programmes and television
theme music.
Prizes: The teams are competing for the title of Telly
Addict of the Year.

Mastermind   BBC Television
Presenter: Magnus Magnusson

Contestants: Eggheads only need apply! In-depth
specialized knowledge on a couple of subjects required.
Superior general knowledge essential!
Game Outline: Four contestants battle it out by
answering questions fired in quick succession
while they are sitting in the 'hot seat'. First round

on the individual's specialized knowledge and
the second round general knowledge. Contestants
have to be aware that the number of 'passes'
may be taken into account when totalling up the
points.

Prizes: Cut glass bowl to the overall series winner.

Appendix 2

Independent

Television

Companies

Anglia Television,
   Anglia House,
   Norwich NR1 3JG
   Tel: 0603 615151

Border Television,
   The Television Centre,
   Carlisle CA1 3NT
   Tel: 0228 25101

Central Independent
   Television,
   Central House,
   Broad Street,
   Birmingham B1 2JP
   Tel: 021–643 9898

Central Independent
   Television,
   East Midlands Television
   Centre,
   Nottingham NG7 2NA
   Tel: 0602 863322

Channel Four Television,
   60 Charlotte Street,
   London W1P 2AX
   Tel: 071–631 4444

Channel Television Ltd.
   Television Centre,
   La Pouquelaye,
   St Helier,
   Jersey,
   Channel Islands,
   Tel: 0534 68999

Grampian Television plc.
   Queen's Cross,
   Aberdeen AB9 2XJ
   Tel: 0224 646464

Granada Television Ltd.
   Granada TV Centre,
   Manchester M60 9EA
   Tel: 061–832 7211

HTV Ltd.
Television Centre,
Culverhouse Cross,
Cardiff CF1 9XL
Tel: 0222 590590

HTV Ltd.
Television Centre,
Bath Road,
Bristol BS4 3HG
Tel: 0272 778366

LWT (London Weekend
Television Ltd.)
South Bank Television
Centre,
London SE1 9LT
Tel: 071–620 1620

S4C (the Welsh Fourth
Channel),
Sophia Close,
Cardiff CF1 9XY
Tel: 0222 343421

Scottish Television plc.
Cowcaddens,
Glasgow G2 3PR
Tel: 041–332 9999

TV-am,
Breakfast Television Centre,
Hawley Crescent,
London NW1 8EF
Tel: 071–267 4300

TVS (Television South) plc.
Television Centre,
Northam,
Southampton SO9 5HZ
Tel: 0703 634211

TVS (Television South) plc.
Television Centre,
Vinters Park,
Maidstone,
Kent ME14 5NZ
Tel: 0622 691111

TSW (Television South-West)
Ltd.
Derrys Cross,
Plymouth PL1 2SP
Tel: 0752 663322

Thames Television plc.
306 Euston Road,
London NW1 3BB
Tel: 071–387 9494

Studios:
Thames Television plc.
Teddington Lock,
Teddington,
Middlesex TW11 9NT
Tel: 081–977 3252

Tyne Tees Television Ltd.
The Television Centre,
City Road,
Newcastle upon Tyne
NE1 2AL
Tel: 091–261 0181

Ulster Television plc.
Havelock House,
Ormeau Road,
Belfast BT7 1EB
Tel: 0232 328122

Yorkshire Television Ltd.
The Television Centre,
Leeds LS3 1JS
Tel: 0532 438283

BBC

For all shows except Mastermind *and* Telly Addicts	BBC Television Contestant Research Dept., Room AG22, 56 Wood Lane, London W12 7RJ *Tel*: 081–743 8000

For Mastermind only, *write to*:	BBC Television, 'Mastermind', PO Box 344, Borehamwood Herts WD6 1AQ

For Telly Addicts only, *write to*:	BBC Television, 'Telly Addicts', BBC Pebble Mill, Birmingham B5 7QQ

Main Address:	BBC Television, Television Centre, Wood Lane, London W12 7RJ *Tel*: 081–743 8000

SATELLITE TELEVISION BROADCASTERS

British Sky Broadcasting plc.
  6 Centaurs Business Park,
  Grant Way,
  Off Syon Lane,
  Isleworth,
  Middlesex TW7 5QD
  Tel: 081–782 3000

MAJOR INDEPENDENT PRODUCTION COMPANIES

Many game shows are now commissioned by broadcast
companies from independent producers. There are
literally scores of independent producers and the major ones

are listed below. If you don't know the name or address of an independent game show producer, contact the television station that transmitted the show you are interested in and they will be able to give you the name, address and telephone number of the production company. Remember that both ITV and BBC use independent production companies. Nearly all shows on satellite television are made by independent producers.

Action Time Ltd.
  Wrendal House,
  2 Whitworth Street West,
  Manchester M1 5WX
  Tel: 061–236 8999

Celador Productions,
  39 Long Acre,
  London WC2E 9JT
  Tel: 071–240 8101

Chapter One Productions,
  Strode House,
  46–48 Osnaburgh Street,
  London NW1 3ND
  Tel: 071–383 4226

Chatsworth Television,
  97/99 Dean Street,

London W1V 5RA
  Tel: 071–434 1731

Noel Gay Television Ltd.
  24 Denmark Street,
  London WC2H 8NJ
  Tel: 071–379 5953

Reg Grundy Productions,
  Enterprise House,
  59–65 Upper Ground,
  London SE1 9PQ
  Tel: 071–928 8942

Regent Productions Ltd.
  The Mews,
  6 Putney Common,
  Putney,
  London SW15 1HL
  Tel: 081–789 5350

Index